NC'L

18 SEP

SHIPWRECKS AROUND BRITAIN
A DIVER'S GUIDE

SHIPWRECKS AROUND BRITAIN

A Diver's Guide

by
Leo Zanelli

With 24 charts and 18 photographs

KAYE & WARD · LONDON

First published by
KAYE & WARD LTD
194–200 Bishopsgate, London EC2
1970

ISBN 0 7182 0866 8

Printed in Great Britain
by Ebenezer Baylis and Son Limited
The Trinity Press, Worcester, and London

INTRODUCTION

Shipwrecks have always excited the imagination, partly because they were inaccessible to the man-in-the-street, a situation that does not apply today. Subaqua divers can now reach, with relative ease, many of the wrecks at the bottom of the seas surrounding Britain; many subaqua clubrooms possess objects of extreme interest such as helms, portholes, etc, from famous vessels, and even items of historical interest. This is not 'underwater piracy', many clubs have purchased their own wrecks, and most clubs have a list of wrecks to visit for their own general diving.

However, although the amount of literature on shipwrecks is increasing, little of it is directed at the only person who could actually visit these wrecks—the diver. The sea is a vast place, and a description of a location which reads 'wrecked several miles SE of the Shambles' is worse than useless to the diver. He needs to know the location as precisely as possible; and even then it is often quite a feat to locate the object.

This book lists some 400 wrecks, mainly within the depths that the club diver reaches and mostly wrecked this century. The locations, in all but a few cases, are extremely accurate. It is not a list of 'treasure' ships, but is aimed at the club diver who participates, or would like to, in the fascinating subject of wreck diving.

I have included some 20% 'unknown' wrecks. These are wrecks that, usually, the Royal Navy survey vessels have located but never identified. Most of them have never been visited, but only 'pinged' on a sounder. These, I think, are the really interesting ones, you never know what you might find! And it is here that the diver can make a valuable contribution to our knowledge. If you should dive on any of these unknown wrecks—whether you discover the name or not—please could I ask you to write and inform me, or the Hydrographer of the Navy, so that the valuable records the department keeps can be corrected. Thank you.

5

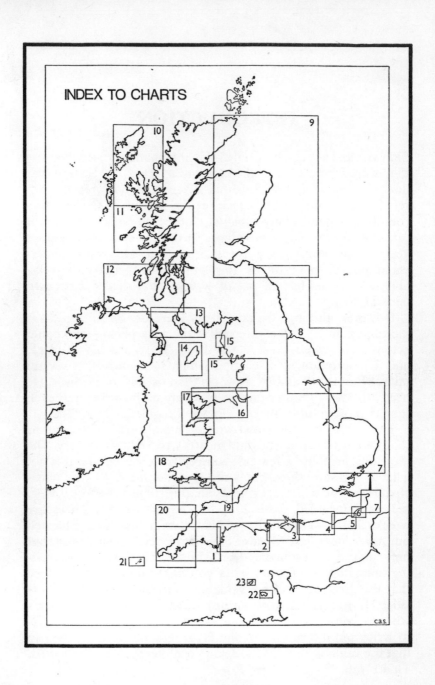

INDEX TO CHARTS

LIST OF CHARTS

This list of charts and the index to charts on the facing page show how the coastline of the British Isles has been divided into areas. There is a detailed chart of each of these areas in the text, showing the location of the shipwrecks, in close proximity to where details are to be found of the wrecks in the particular chart.

PHOTOGRAPHS

(between pages 56 and 57)

1 Artist's impression of the Bretagne (wreck 32) drawn from general arrangements drawings supplied by the shipbuilders. Artist: John Brown.

2 Bell of the Bretagne, recovered by divers of the Bristol Aeroplane Brance of the BSAC. Photo: G. Troote.

3 Recovered from the Bretagne by the same divers. A Pelorus? It was hung in a gimbal, probably on the bridge. The base is lead filled to assist stability. Photo: G. Troote.

4 Recovered from the Bretagne, also by the same divers. A coat hanger, possibly from the captain's quarters; and a telegraph handle, the wood of which is in very good condition compared to that of other woods found nearby. Photo: G. Troote.

5 The Lady Charlotte (wreck 372) aground on Porthellick Point. Photo: Gibson.

6 Drawing of the SS Schiller (wreck 362).

7 The MV Mando (wreck 379) on Golden Ball Bar. Photo: Gibson.

8 The Earl of Lonsdale (wreck 365). Photo: Gibson.

9 The King Cadwallon (wreck 380). Photo: Gibson.

10 The Serica (wreck 369). Photo: Gibson.

11 The Minnehaha (wreck 370). Photo Gibson.

12 The submarine M2 (wreck 44) shown here after alterations to carry a seaplane.

13 The armed merchant cruiser Otranto (wreck 205).

14 HMS Ariadne (wreck 107).

15 HMS Falmouth (wreck 162).

16 HMS Argyll (wreck 176).

17 HMS Campania (wreck 172) after alterations with twin funnels forward.

18 HMS Campania, sinking.

(Photos 12–18 incl.: Imperial War Museum.)

ACKNOWLEDGEMENTS

I gratefully acknowledge the assistance given me by the Hydrographer of the Royal Navy, Rear Admiral G. S. Ritchie, CB, DSc, FRICS and his Department. And to Mr and Mrs S. Craig, who drew the excellent charts which are a feature of this book. Also, if this book is in any measure successful, a large share of the credit must go to Alec Reynolds of the Hydrographic Department; Alec participated at every stage and was a tower of strength and information—without his help this would have been a very different and, I think, less comprehensive publication.

ABBREVIATIONS & MEANINGS

Dimensions: In feet—length × beam × draught
Route: At date of sinking
Bottom: Average depth from water surface to sea bed
Least: Least depth from water surface to top of wreck
Height: Height of wreck from sea bed
t.g.: Tons gross
t.n.: Tons net
t.d.: Tons displacement
(E): Exact position
(A): Approximate position
HSF: Horizontal sextant fixes
B & D: Bearing and distance

9

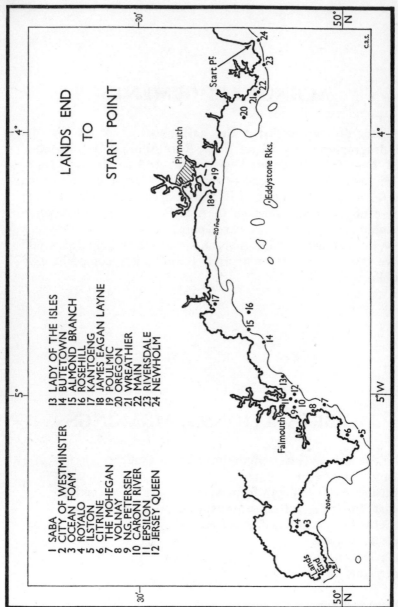

LANDS END

TO

START POINT

1 SABA
2 CITY OF WESTMINSTER
3 OCEAN FOAM
4 ROYALO
5 ILSTON
6 CITRINE
7 THE MOHEGAN
8 VOLNAY
9 N.G. PETERSEN
10 CARONI RIVER
11 EPSILON
12 JERSEY QUEEN
13 LADY OF THE ISLES
14 BUTETOWN
15 ALMOND BRANCH
16 ROSEHILL
17 KANTOENG
18 JAMES EAGAN LAYNE
19 POULMIC
20 OREGON
21 WREATHIER
22 MAIN
23 RIVERSDALE
24 NEWHOLM

Chart 1   Land's End to Start Point

Wreck 1. The Dutch mv SABA

DIMENSIONS: 148 × 25 × 9·5.   TONNAGE: 400 t.g.
CARGO: 500 t. high grade steel.   SINKING: 21st April 1966.
LOCATION: lat 50° 01′ 57″ N. long 05° 40′ 05″ W. (E).
DEPTH: bottom 46′–54′.   SURVEYS: Trinity House 1966 and 1969; subaqua 1969.
ADDITIONAL: The Trinity House survey of 1967 reported that 'The wreck is badly broken up.' Subaqua divers in 1969 gave the following information: 'Wreck is in three parts, the bow is upside down, the stern lying on the starboard side and the wreckage is strewn amongst the rocks, some of which are higher than the wreck itself.'

Wreck 2. British steamship CITY OF WESTMINSTER

DIMENSIONS: 470·5 × 62·1 × 25·2.   TONNAGE: 6094 t.g.
BUILT: 1916 by Flensburg Schiff S.B. Gest.
ROUTE: Belfast–Rotterdam.   CARGO: maize.
OWNERS: City of Oran Steamship Co.
SINKING: 8th October 1923.
LOCATION: lat 50° 01′ 30″ N. long 05° 40′ 08″ W. (E).
DEPTH: bottom 120′.
ADDITIONAL: The CoW hit the Runnel Stone at 3 p.m. and effectively removed the tip of the Stone. After breaking its back the CoW slipped off and sank. Original name—RUDELSBURG.

Wreck 3. HMS OCEAN FOAM

TONNAGE: 90 t.g.   SINKING: 6th October 1918.
LOCATION: lat 50° 05′ 12″ N. long 05° 30′ 47″ W. (A).
DEPTH: bottom 90′.
ADDITIONAL: This vessel was a drifter requisitioned at the outbreak of World War One. Sunk by collision, this wreck, as far as is known, has never been located although the estimated position is said to be reasonably accurate.

Wreck 4. Minesweeper HMS ROYALO

TONNAGE: 248 t.g.   SINKING: 1st September 1940.

11

LOCATION: lat 50° 06′ 46″ N. long 05° 30′ 56″ W. (E).
DEPTH: least 14′. SURVEYS: RN 1965, subaqua 1967.
ADDITIONAL: A minesweeper, the Royalo was ironically sunk by a mine. Formerly a Grimsby trawler, it was requisitioned in 1939. The RN survey states 'Wreck is 82′ long, and appears to have had its stern blown off. Highest point is a davit standing up on the bows.' The subaqua report indicates 'Boilers still intact, as are some of the deck cabins. A good dive.'

Wreck 5. British steamship ILSTON
DIMENSIONS: 300 × 44 × 18·75. TONNAGE: 2426 t.g.
BUILT: 1915. CARGO: railway equipment.
OWNERS: Swansea Steamers. SINKING: 30th April 1917.
LOCATION: lat 49° 57′ 00″ N. long 05° 09′ 36″ W.
DEPTH: bottom 165′. SURVEYS: subaqua.
ADDITIONAL: Torpedoed by a German submarine. Divers located this wreck in 1969 and reported that 'The wreck is lying intact, bows pointing SW. All the cargo is still in the holds and the engines are still intact.' The divers only had one dive on the remains and, on subsequent dives later in the year, were unable to re-locate it.

Wreck 6. British steamship CITRINE
TONNAGE: 788 t.g. CARGO: limestone.
SINKING: 2nd January 1956.
LOCATION: lat 49° 59′ 17″ N. long 05° 09′ 35″ W. (A). 3·5 miles from the Lizard Light.
ADDITIONAL: Foundered and sank in a storm.

Wreck 7. Cargo liner MOHEGAN
DIMENSIONS: 482 × 52 × 34·5. TONNAGE: 8500 t.g.
BUILT: 1898 by Earle's Shipbuilding Co.
ROUTE: Gravesend–New York. CARGO: 150 t. jute, tin and linoleum. OWNERS: Atlantic Transport Line.
SINKING: 14th October 1898
LOCATION: lat 50° 02′ 43″ N. long 05° 02′ 36″ W. (E).
DEPTH: bottom 70′, least 50′. SURVEYS: subaqua.
ADDITIONAL: Originally launched as the CLEOPATRA, the Mohegan was not one year old when it sank. The site was located by divers in 1961 who reported: 'Boilers are in centre of wreck, which lies N–S. Some wreckage strewn about. Ribs are

12

15' high on the sea bed. An excellent dive.' This is a popular dive with experienced divers.

Wreck 8. Armed British merchant steamship VOLNAY
DIMENSIONS: 385 × 52 × 26.   TONNAGE: 4610 t.g.
ROUTE: Montreal–Plymouth.
CARGO: ammunition and luxury goods.
OWNERS: Gow Harrison & Co.   SINKING: 14th December 1917.
LOCATION: lat 50° 04' 15" N. long 05° 04' 03" W. (E).
DEPTH: bottom 57'.   SURVEYS: subaqua.
ADDITIONAL: A diver's report in 1967 stated 'Cargo of ammunition partly salvaged. Two large boilers intact, bows intact.' In fact, at this date about one sixth of the cargo remained, some of it strewn about the sea bed.

Wreck 9. Danish steamship N. G. PETERSEN
DIMENSIONS: 239 × 36·2 × 19.   TONNAGE: 1282 t.g. 803 t.n.
BUILT: 1898 of steel.   CARGO: 1900 t. iron ore.
OWNERS: sub-chartered to Furness Whitby Co.
SINKING: 13th March 1918.
LOCATION: lat 50° 07' 04" N. long 05° 03' 04" W. (E).
DEPTH: least 51'.   SURVEYS: HMS Medusa 1960.
ADDITIONAL: Sunk by collision. Survey reports 'Wreck lying NNW by SSE; no scour.'

Wreck 10. Tanker CARONI RIVER
TONNAGE: 7807 t.g.   SINKING: 20th June 1940.
LOCATION: lat 50° 06' 59" N. long 05° 01' 52" W. (E).
DEPTH: bottom 60'.   SURVEYS: RN and subaqua.
ADDITIONAL: Sunk by mine. Subaqua report of 1969 states 'The remains of a trawler are intermingled with the Caroni River, which has been blown and lies in three main parts.'

Wreck 11. Dutch vessel EPSILON
DIMENSIONS: 331·7 × 48 × 22·2.   TONNAGE 3211 t.g.
BUILT: 1913.   SINKING: 31st January 1917.
LOCATION: lat 50° 07' 37" N. long 05° 01' 24" W. (E) Or, HSF Trehunsey Jean 79° 34' to Pendennis Castle 70° 13' to St Anthony's Coastguard Station.
DEPTH: least 58'.   HEIGHT: 15'.
SURVEYS: HMS Medusa 1960, subaqua 1969.
ADDITIONAL: Sunk by mine. Medusa survey indicated that the wreck is lying NE and there is a small 2' scour. Subaqua report

13

'Located in charted position using sextant and grapnel. Wreck has been heavily dispersed but engines still stand 15' proud of the sea bed. Boilers, twisted girders and rest of wreckage stands some 12' high on a bed of sand. A very good dive.'

Wreck 12. British merchant steamship JERSEY QUEEN
TONNAGE: 910 t.g.   SINKING: 6th October 1940.
LOCATION: lat 50° 07' 10" N. long 05° 00' 09" W. (A).
SURVEYS: Trinity House and HMS Scott.
ADDITIONAL: As far as is known, this wreck has never been located. The position given is that stated by Falmouth Coastguard Station at the time of loss and should be reasonably accurate. Although two search/surveys have been carried out they were hampered by the rocky nature of the sea bed. The wreck could easily be amongst rocks as the depths vary from 56' to 84'.

Wreck 13. HMS LADY OF THE ISLES
TONNAGE: 166 t.g.   SINKING 3rd October 1940.
DEPTH: bottom 60'.
LOCATION: lat 50° 09' 00" N. long 04° 56' 00" W. (A).
ADDITIONAL: A requisitioned vessel used as a cable ship, this wreck has never been located.

Wreck 14. Armed British merchant steamship BUTE TOWN
TONNAGE: 1829 t.g.   SINKING: 29th January 1918.
LOCATION: lat 50° 11' 42" N. long 04° 48' 00" W. (A).
ADDITIONAL: Torpedoed. This wreck has never been located although the position should be reasonably accurate.

Wreck 15. Armed British merchant steamship ALMOND BRANCH
TONNAGE: 3461 t.g.   BUILT: 1897.
ROUTE: London–S. America via Port Talbot.   CARGO: general.
SINKING: 27th November 1917.
LOCATION: lat 50° 14' 00" N. long 04° 45' 00" W. (A).
ADDITIONAL: Former name ASHMORE. Torpedoed. This wreck has never been located.

Wreck 16. Armed British merchant steamship ROSE HILL
TONNAGE: 2788 t.g.   ROUTE: Cardiff–Devonport.
CARGO: coal.   SINKING: 23rd September 1917.
LOCATION: lat 50° 15' N. long 04° 41' W. (A) (see below).
DEPTH: bottom 140'.   SURVEYS: HMS Woodlark 1966.

ADDITIONAL: The 1966 survey located a wreck in exact position lat 50° 14′ 00″ N, long 04° 41′ 12″ W. From information received it is assumed that this is the Rose Hill. The wreck located stands some 30′ high in 140′ of water.

Wreck 17. Dredger KANTOENG
SINKING: April 1937.
DEPTH: bottom 43′, least 23′.   HEIGHT: 20′.
LOCATION: lat 50° 18′ 55″ N. long 04° 38′ 03″ W. (E). Or, HSF Cribben Head Daymark 101° 04′ to Fowey Head Lighthouse, this being in transit at 33° 36′ to right-hand chimney of a conspicuous white house and Fowey Lighthouse is in transit with Fowey County Secondary School.
SURVEYS: subaqua.
ADDITIONAL: This wreck was discovered by divers who reported 'The "A" frame is lying flat, the large bucket chain and wreckage stand 20′ high lying in an E–W direction.'

Wreck 18. American Liberty ship JAMES EGAN LAYNE
TONNAGE: 7176 t.g.   CARGO: engineering stores, 6000 t.
SINKING: 21st March 1945.
LOCATION: lat 50° 19′ 32″ N. long 04° 04′ 41″ W. (E).
DEPTH: bottom 80′.   SURVEYS: subaqua.
ADDITIONAL: This has probably been the most dived-on wreck in Britain. Lying upright on a sandy bed, the James E. Layne is now dangerous owing to salvage. The engines are precariously balanced and the mast is insecure.

Wreck 19. POULMIC
SINKING: 9th November 1940.
LOCATION: lat 50° 18′ 54″ N. long 04° 10′ 06″ W. (A).
ADDITIONAL: This wreck has never been located.

Wreck 20. OREGON
TONNAGE: 801 t.g.   CARGO: nitrate of soda.
SINKING: 18th December 1890.
LOCATION: lat 50° 14′ 36″ N. long 03° 56′ 30″ W. (E).
DEPTH: bottom 150′.   SURVEYS: subaqua, 1967.
ADDITIONAL: This wreck was discovered by divers. At the time of loss, the position given was 'Off Bolt Tail in Bigbury Bay.' In 1966 divers reported 'Located a wreck in position (above) approx. 120′ long and 20′ beam. Bows fairly intact. Lying in 150′. Slightly disintegrated but quite good condition. Hull is

15

steel and a plate has been removed from wheelhouse with date 1875 on it. Research indicates that this is the Oregon.'

Wreck 21. Armed British steamship WREATHIER
DIMENSIONS: 200 × 31·2 × 12·8. TONNAGE: 852 t.g.
BUILT: 1897 of steel. CARGO: coal.
OWNERS: Adams Allan & Co. SINKING: 3rd December 1917.
LOCATION: lat 50° 13′ 00″ N. long 03° 51′ 00″ W. (A).
SURVEYS: subaqua.
ADDITIONAL: This wreck has never been located precisely. An undated divers' report stated 'No wreck found in this position; but there is one approx. 1 mile SE of this position. This could be the Wreathier.'

Wreck 22. British steamship MAIN
TONNAGE: 3616 t.g. BUILT: 1905. ROUTE: London–Philadelphia.
CARGO: 500 t. chalk, 50 t. cowhair, horsehair, goatskins, and fenugreek seeds.
OWNERS: Atlantic Transport Co. SINKING: 23rd March 1917.
LOCATION: lat 50° 12′ 45″ N. long 03° 50′ 53″ W. (E).
DEPTH: bottom 120′. SURVEYS: subaqua.
ADDITIONAL: This wreck is owned by Torbay BSAC, who discovered it.

Wreck 23. Armed British merchant steamship RIVERSDALE
TONNAGE: 2805 t.g. ROUTE: Tyne–Sevonia.
CARGO: coal. SINKING: 18th December 1917.
LOCATION: lat 50° 11′ 42″ N. long 03° 44′ 03″ W. (E).
DEPTH: least 104′. HEIGHT: 46′. SURVEYS: subaqua.
ADDITIONAL: Virtually intact on an even keel, lying on sand. Very strong tidal streams. For experienced divers only. This wreck is owned by Torbay BSAC.

Wreck 24. Armed British steamship NEWHOLM
DIMENSIONS: 330 × 48 × 23·5. TONNAGE: 3399 t.g.
BUILT: 1899 by C. S. Swan & Hunter. CARGO: iron ore.
OWNERS: J. J. & C. M. Foster. SINKING: 8th September 1917.
LOCATION: lat 50° 12′ 32″ N. long 03° 38′ 24″ W. (E).
DEPTH: bottom 110′, least 66′.
SURVEYS: HMS Scott 1967, subaqua 1968.
ADDITIONAL: The subaqua reports read 'Wreck is lying at an angle of 30° with a list to starboard, in a shoal. It is stuck into the sandbank on which it rests; so much so that the sand is only

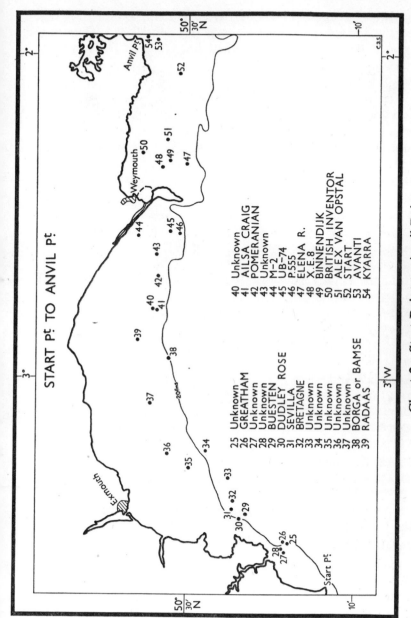

START Pt. TO ANVIL Pt.

25 Unknown	40 Unknown
26 GREATHAM	41 AILSA CRAIG
27 Unknown	42 POMERANIAN
28 Unknown	43 Unknown
29 BUESTEN	44 M-2
30 DUDLEY ROSE	45 UB-74
31 SEVILLA	46 P.555
32 BRETAGNE	47 ELENA R.
33 Unknown	48 X.E.8
34 Unknown	49 BINNENDIJK
35 Unknown	50 BRITISH INVENTOR
36 Unknown	51 ALEX VAN OPSTAL
37 Unknown	52 START
38 BORGA or BAMSE	53 AVANTI
39 RADAAS	54 KYARRA

Chart 2   Start Point to Anvil Point

B

17

just short of the starboard bulwarks. The hull is badly broken, and the first 60' of the bow is completely demolished. The whole wreck is alive with marine life of all descriptions.' The Newholm was sunk by a mine.

Wreck 25. Unknown
LOCATION: lat 50° 17' 58" N. long 03° 30' 30" W. (E).
SURVEYS: HMS Gleaner 1939; HMS Seagull 1950.
ADDITIONAL: This wreck was first located by HMS Gleaner immediately before World War Two. The latest report is by HMS Seagull in 1950; this indicated that the wreck was a substantial one as it stood 25' high on the sea bed in general depths of 90'.

Wreck 26. British steamship GREATHAM
TONNAGE: 2338 t.g.   BUILT: 1890 of iron.
CARGO: coal.   SINKING: 2nd January 1918.
LOCATION: lat 50° 18' 15" N. long 03° 30' 21" W. (E).
HSF: Start Point Lighthouse 102° 54' to the Day Beacon 40° 03' to Berry Head Lighthouse.
DEPTH: bottom 110'–120', least 94'. SURVEYS: HMS Scott 1952.
ADDITIONAL: Apart from the above information, HMS Scott reported that the remains of the wreck are 300' in length. Former name BOUORAH.

Wreck 27. Unknown
LOCATION: lat 50° 18' 20" N. long 03° 32' 11" W. (E).
SURVEYS: HMS Seagull 1950.
ADDITIONAL: First located by HMS Seagull in the 1950 survey. Average depths are 110' and the wreck stands 20' high.

Wreck 28. Unknown
LOCATION: lat 50° 18' 29" N. long 03° 31' 38" W. (E).
SURVEYS: HMS Seagull 1950.
ADDITIONAL: This also was located by HMS Seagull in 1950. The wreck stands some 21' high in general depths of 100'.

Wreck 29. Norwegian tanker BUESTEN
DIMENSIONS: 388·1 × 52·7 × 29.   TONNAGE: 5187 t.g.
BUILT: 1927.   SINKING: 9th April 1941.   CARGO: in the 5 aft tanks—benzine, in the 3 forward tanks—kerosene.
LOCATION: lat 50° 22' 49" N. long 03° 25' 15" W. (E).
DEPTH: bottom 125'.   HEIGHT: 25'.
SURVEYS: HMS Seagull 1950.

18

ADDITIONAL: The information relating to the height of the wreck and general depth was obtained during the 1950 survey.

Wreck 30. British steamship DUDLEY ROSE
TONNAGE: 1600 t.g.   SINKING: 9th April 1941.
LOCATION: lat 50° 23′ 38″ N. long 03° 26′ 15″ W. (E).
DEPTH: bottom 90′.   HEIGHT: 31′.
SURVEYS: HMS Seagull 1950; subaqua 1960.
ADDITIONAL: The subaqua report stated 'It lies on an even keel virtually intact, though the bridge is badly damaged.' Another, unconfirmed, subaqua report stated 'There is a cylindrical metal object, something like a bomb, under the bridge.'

Wreck 31. Steamship SEVILLA
TONNAGE: 1318 t.g.   SINKING: 25th April 1918.
LOCATION: lat 50° 24′ 25″ N. long 03° 24′ 29″ W. (E).
DEPTH: bottom 95′.   HEIGHT: 30′.   SURVEYS: subaqua 1964.
ADDITIONAL: The subaqua report stated that the wreck, though dived on, was not properly examined. It is lying on an even keel with the hull probably intact although well silted up. There is no trace of either rudder or propeller.

Wreck 32. Norwegian steamship schooner BRETAGNE
DIMENSIONS: 231·6 × 35·2 × 14·7.   TONNAGE: 1382 t.g. 860 t.n.
BUILT: 1903.   OWNERS: Fred Olsen Lines.
SINKING: 10th August 1918.
LOCATION: lat 50° 24′ 17″ N. long 03° 22′ 48″ W. (E).
DEPTH: bottom 100′.   SURVEYS: HMS Seagull; subaqua.
ADDITIONAL: Engines, triple expansion. Sail area 2000 sq ft approx. This wreck has been purchased by the Bristol Aeroplane Company Branch of the BSAC.

Wreck 33. Unknown
LOCATION: lat 50° 24′ 56″ N. long 03° 18′ 43″ W. (E).
DEPTH: bottom 95′.   HEIGHT: 43′.   SURVEYS: HMS Seagull 1951.
ADDITIONAL: This wreck was located by HMS Seagull. As can be seen from the scant information available, this was a large vessel. Some reports say that this is the steamship GRELEEN, of 2286 t.g. sunk in World War One.

Wreck 34. Unknown
LOCATION: lat 50° 27′ 39″ N. long 03° 13′ 45″ W. (E).
DEPTH: bottom 130′.   HEIGHT: 41′.
SURVEYS: HMS Seagull 1950; subaqua.

ADDITIONAL: As with the previous wreck, this was obviously a large vessel, and well worth looking for. The subaqua report only says that it is 'Probably a 1914–18 wreck', but does not indicate whether it was actually dived on.

Wreck 35. Unknown
LOCATION: lat 50° 29' 34" N. long 03° 16' 55" W. (E).
DEPTH: bottom 90'.   SURVEYS: RN 1938; subaqua 1964.
ADDITIONAL: This wreck was located in 1938. The subaqua report stated that the vessel lies on an even keel, the hull apparently intact and is of a small coaster type. A small gun was seen on the stern.

Wreck 36. Unknown
LOCATION: lat 50° 32' 10" N. long 03° 14' 12" W. (E).
DEPTH: bottom 90'.   HEIGHT: 30'.
SURVEYS: RN 1938; HMS Scott 1952.
ADDITIONAL: The wreck is some 300' long, lying on a bed of fine sand. First located in 1938, some reports say that this is the steamship BOMBA of 2694 t.g. Lying in a WNW by ESE direction.

Wreck 37. Unknown
LOCATION: lat 50° 34' 12" N. long 03° 04' 48" W. (E).
DEPTH: bottom 80'.   SURVEYS: RN; subaqua 1964.
ADDITIONAL: This wreck was first located in 1917. The subaqua report states that the wreck is well broken up and dispersed over a large area with little chance of identification. The bottom is sand and shell over chalk.

Wreck 38. BAMSE (or BORGA)
TONNAGE: 1046 t.g.   SINKING: 1st March 1918.
LOCATION: lat 50° 32' 03" N. long 02° 56' 33" W. (E).
DEPTH: bottom 124', least 113'.   SURVEYS: HMS Scott 1952.
ADDITIONAL: The survey indicated that the bottom was very hard sand with a very fine sand covering. The wreck lies NW by SE and is about 200' long.

Wreck 39. Danish steamship RADAAS
TONNAGE: 2524 t.g.   SINKING: 21st September 1917.
LOCATION: lat 50° 35' 49" N. long 02° 53' 00" W. (E).
DEPTH: bottom 90'.   SURVEYS: RN.
ADDITIONAL: It is not certain that this is the Radaas. A RN survey located the wreck in the position the Radaas went down

in and it is assumed to be correct. 300' in length, lying NNE by SSW.

Wreck 40. Unknown
LOCATION: lat 50° 33' 58" N. long 02° 47' 15" W. (E).
DEPTH: bottom 95'. HEIGHT: 30'. SURVEYS: HMS Scott 1952.
ADDITIONAL: The survey reports that this wreck is 300' in length, lying NE by SW. It is thought that it may be a submarine, but this requires subaqua confirmation. This is only two cables NE from wreck 41.

Wreck 41. Steamship AILSA CRAIG
TONNAGE: 601 t.g. ROUTE: Cardiff–Weymouth.
CARGO: coal. SINKING: 15th April 1918.
LOCATION: lat 50° 33' 58" N. long 02° 47' 15" W. (E).
DEPTH: bottom 100', least 78'. SURVEYS: HMS Scott 1952.
ADDITIONAL: The survey reported that the wreck was 200' long, lying NE by SW. This is only two cables SW from Wreck 40.

Wreck 42. British steamship POMERANIAN
DIMENSIONS: 381 × 43·8 × 33. TONNAGE: 4241 t.g. 2694 t.n.
BUILT: 1880 of iron. CARGO: listed as 'general Government'.
SINKING: 15th April 1918.
LOCATION: lat 50° 33' 30" N. long 02° 41' 23" W. (E).
DEPTH: bottom 100', least 74'. SURVEYS: HMS Scott 1952.
ADDITIONAL: This was a liner requisitioned from Canadian Pacific Ocean Services for use in World War One. Surveys indicate that the wreck is lying NW by SE and is 350' long.

Wreck 43. Unknown
LOCATION: lat 50° 33' 43" N. long 02° 37' 28" W. (E).
DEPTH: bottom 105', least 80'.
SURVEYS: RN 1932; HMS Scott 1952.
ADDITIONAL: This wreck was first located in the 1932 survey. The latest survey states that it is lying NW by SE and is 350' long.

Wreck 44. British 'M' class submarine M.2
DIMENSIONS: length 296', beam 24·5'. TONNAGE: 1650 t.d.
BUILT: 1918 by Vickers. SINKING: 1932.
LOCATION: lat 50° 34' 35" N. long 02° 33' 56" W. (E).
DEPTH: bottom 85', least 65'. SURVEYS: Regularly (see below).
ADDITIONAL: The M2 had diesel engines (2 screws, 2400/1600 bhp, 15·5/9·5 knots) and carried a complement of 60–70 officers and men. Originally designed to carry a single 12" gun, in 1927 the

submarine was altered to carry a seaplane. In 1932 the vessel submerged with the hangar doors open, foundering and losing all hands. Latest surveys indicate that it is lying N by S, the southern end shallowest. It is used as a training target for naval sonar operators. Some salvage operations were carried out in 1932–33.

Wreck 45. German 'UB III' class submarine UB74
DIMENSIONS: length 182', beam 19'. TONNAGE: 508/650 t.d.
BUILT: 1917. SINKING: 26th May 1918.
LOCATION: lat 50° 32' 01" N. long 02° 33' 04" W. (E). Or, HSF Black Down (Hardy Mont) 67° 25' to Verne Radar 39° 52' to Portland Bill Lighthouse.
DEPTH: bottom 86'. SURVEYS: RN.
ADDITIONAL: The UB.74 had diesel engines (2 screws, 1100/788 bhp, 13·5/7·5 knots). The latest survey reports that it is lying NE by SW.

Wreck 46. Submarine P555
DIMENSIONS: 219 × 20 × 16. TONNAGE: 854 t.d.
BUILT: 1922 in Bethlehem, USA. SINKING: 25th August 1947.
LOCATION: lat 50° 30' 52" N. long 02° 33' 27" W. (E).
DEPTH: least 101'. SURVEYS: Regular (sonar target).
ADDITIONAL: This was formerly the USN submarine S24. It was sunk on the above date for use as a target vessel for sonar operators. Surveys state that the wreck is 300' long with a small 2' scour.

Wreck 47. Greek steamship ELENA R
DIMENSIONS: 370 × 53·2 × 27. TONNAGE: 4576 t.g.
BUILT: 1917 by Newport Steamship & Dry Docking.
SINKING: 22nd November 1939.
LOCATION: lat 50° 30' 12" N. long 02° 20' 37" W. (E).
DEPTH: bottom 80'. SURVEYS: RN survey ship FSL Waterwitch.
ADDITIONAL: The survey report states that a ridge of broken shell now unites the position of the wreck to the Shambles Bank, which is half a mile westward. It is considered probable that this bank has been formed as a result of eddies, etc, in the tidal streams initiated by the wreck itself. Apart from being of interest to oceanologists, this 'memorial ridge' should make the wreck easy to locate. The Elena R, according to the survey, is presumed to have broken up or be breaking up.

Wreck 48. Midget submarine XE8
DIMENSIONS: length 53', beam 5·75'.   TONNAGE: 30/34 t.
SINKING: 3rd November 1954.
LOCATION: lat 50° 33' 01" N. long 02° 21' 06" W. (E).
DEPTH: bottom 78'.   SURVEYS: RN.
ADDITIONAL: The engine was a single-shaft diesel/electric (42/
30 bhp, 6·5/6 knots) with a complement of 4 or 5. This vessel
was lost whilst on tow. Latest surveys state that the wreck is
very difficult to locate owing to the irregular sea bed in the area.

Wreck 49. Dutch steamship BINNENDIJK
DIMENSIONS: 400·4 × 54·3 × 36·6.   TONNAGE: 6873 t.g.
BUILT: 1921.   SINKING: 8th September 1939.
OWNERS: Holland America Line.
LOCATION: lat 50° 32' 07" N. long 02° 20' 00" W. (E).
DEPTH: bottom 90', least 53'.   SURVEYS: RN 1949.
ADDITIONAL: The 1949 survey reported that the wreck is some
500' long. It is reported that some minor salvage took place in
1952.

Wreck 50. British tanker, steamship BRITISH INVENTOR
TONNAGE: 11,600 t.dw. 7101 t.g.   ROUTE: Abadan–UK.
CARGO: oil.   SINKING: 13th June 1940.
LOCATION: lat 50° 35' 20" N. long 02° 18' 30" W. (E).
DEPTH: approx. 58'.   SURVEYS: RN.
ADDITIONAL: Only the fore part of the British Inventor was
sunk—the stern part was towed to Southampton and salvaged.
The latest reports state that the wreck is very difficult to locate
owing to the many rock pinnacles existing in the area.

Wreck 51. Belgian motor vessel ALEX VAN OPSTAL
TONNAGE: 5964 t.g.   SINKING: 15th September 1939.
LOCATION: lat 50° 32' 26" N. long 02° 16' 00" W. (E). Or,
HSF Portland Bill Lighthouse 87° 46' to Admiralty Navigation
Beacon 88° 39' to St Aldelm's Church (chapel).
DEPTH: bottom 90', least 58'.   SURVEYS: FSL Waterwitch.
ADDITIONAL: The survey indicated that the wreck was some 500'
long, lying approx 166°/346° with the highest part about one
third from the southern end. The bottom consists of sand,
broken shell and gravel and there is a small scour of between
3'–6'. This wreck has been the target of at least five subaqua
expeditions at the time of writing—all without success.

Wreck 52. Steamship START
DIMENSIONS: 203·8 × 29·1 × 10·7. TONNAGE: 728 t.g. 341 t.n.
BUILT: 1896 of steel, by Scott & Sons. CARGO: coal.
SINKING: 22nd December 1917.
LOCATION: lat 50° 31′ 00″ N. long 02° 03′ 40″ W. (A).
DEPTH: bottom 90′–100′.
ADDITIONAL: As far as is known, this wreck has never been located. But an unconfirmed report by a lone diver states that he has dived on an unknown wreck approx. 300 yd NE of the above position—and this might well be the Start.

Wreck 53. Steamship AVANTI
DIMENSIONS: 272·7 × 40 × 21·1. TONNAGE: 2128 t.g.
SINKING: 2nd February 1918.
LOCATION: lat 50° 33′ 35″ N. long 01° 57′ 15″ W. (E).
DEPTH: bottom 96′. SURVEYS: RN.
ADDITIONAL: It is not known for certain that this is the Avanti. A RN survey ship has located a wreck in this position and, as this was the position given when it went down, it is likely that this is the Avanti.

Wreck 54. Armed British merchant steamship KYARRA
DIMENSIONS: 415 × 52 × 28·6. TONNAGE: 6953 t.g. 4383 t.n.
BUILT: 1903, of steel, by W. Denny & Bros.
SINKING: 6th May 1918.
LOCATION: lat 50° 34′ 53″ N. long 01° 56′ 33″ W. (E)
DEPTH: bottom 92′, least 62′. SURVEYS: subaqua.
ADDITIONAL: The Kyarra remained unlocated until 1966, when a subaqua diver discovered it. The site had been recorded on Admiralty charts as a shoal sounding of 92′, but the diver, who knew the area, was convinced that there were no shoal patches in this area and investigated. Research confirmed that this was the Kyarra, a liner requisitioned from the Australasian Steam Navigation Co. and used as a hospital ship until torpedoed. This wreck is now owned by Kingston BSAC; a member of this club is the (lady) diver who found the wreck.

Wreck 55. Unknown
LOCATION: lat 50° 29′ 00″ N. long 01° 54′ 00″ W. (A).
DEPTH: bottom 72′. SURVEYS: RN 1918.
ADDITIONAL: This mystery wreck was first located in 1918, but

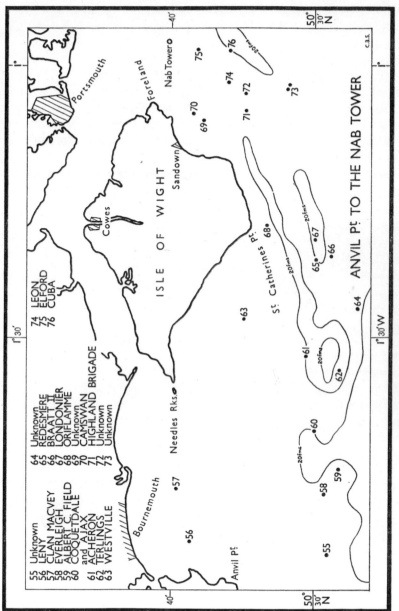

55 Unknown
56 LENY
57 CLAN MACVEY
58 EVERLEIGH
59 ALBERT C. FIELD
60 COQUETDALE
   and AJAX
61 ACHERON
62 TERLINGS
63 WESTVILLE

64 Unknown
65 REDESMERE
66 BRAATT II
67 LONDONIER
68 ORIFLAMME
69 Unknown
70 CAMSWAN
71 HIGHLAND BRIGADE
72 Unknown
73 Unknown

74 LEON
75 ELFORD
76 CUBA

Chart 3   Anvil Point to the Nab Tower

25

this does not mean that it was a war loss. No further surveys have been carried out since.

Wreck 56. Dutch motor vessel LENY
TONNAGE: 343 t.g. SINKING: 23rd June 1942.
LOCATION: lat 50° 38′ 46″ N. long 01° 52′ 31″ W. (E).
DEPTH: bottom 45′. SURVEYS: RN; subaqua 1968.
ADDITIONAL: The RN surveys report that the wreck is broken up and now stands only 2′ high. The subaqua report reads 'Wreck is well broken up and scattered over a large area, but still makes a very interesting dive.'

Wreck 57. Armed British merchant steamship CLAN MACVEY
DIMENSIONS: 400 × 53 × 32·8. TONNAGE: 5815 t.g. 3710 t.n.
BUILT: 1918, of steel, by Northumberland SB Co. CARGO: coal.
OWNERS: Clan Line. SINKING: 8th August 1918.
LOCATION: lat 50° 39′ 40″ N. long 01° 46′ 44″ W. (E).
DEPTH: bottom 45′. HEIGHT: 8′.
SURVEYS: RN; subaqua 1968.
ADDITIONAL: The subaqua report confirmed the position and stated that the wreckage was strewn over a wide area.

Wreck 58. Steamship EVERLEIGH
DIMENSIONS: 406·3 × 56 × 26·9 TONNAGE: 5222 t.g.
SINKING: 6th February 1945.
LOCATION: lat 50° 29′ 16″ N. long 01° 47′ 06″ W. (E).
DEPTH: bottom 120′–130′. HEIGHT: 60′. SURVEYS: RN.
ADDITIONAL: This wreck stands at an enormous height and, as such, should well be worth a visit. As far as the records show there have been no salvage attempts.

Wreck 59. Steamship ALBERT C. FIELD
TONNAGE: 1764 t.g. CARGO: ammunition.
SINKING: 18th June 1944.
LOCATION: lat 50° 28′ 15″ N. long 01° 44′ 44″ W. (E).
DEPTH: bottom 112′. HEIGHT: 12′. SURVEYS: HMS Scott 1955.
ADDITIONAL: This wreck was first located by HMS Scott in the 1955 survey. The report indicates that the bottom is sand, stone and shell. It may be that the wreck is lying at the side of a hole or scour. Further, it would appear that the Albert C. Field is either in two parts—large and small—or there is another, smaller, wreck adjacent. In any case, in view of the cargo it is wise to stay clear.

Wreck 60. Dutch steamship AJAX
TONNAGE: 942 t.g. SINKING: 8th August 1940.
LOCATION: lat 50° 30′ 02″ N. long 01° 40′ 21″ W. (E).
DEPTH: bottom 112′. HEIGHT: 20′. SURVEYS: RN.
ADDITIONAL: This position is actually the combined wreckage of two vessels—the Ajax and the Coquetdale (Wreck 60a). They were both sunk in the same action.

Wreck 60a. British steamship COQUETDALE
TONNAGE: 1597 t.g. (see data on Wreck 60).

Wreck 61. HM destroyer ACHERON
DIMENSIONS: 323 × 32 × 12. TONNAGE: 1350 t.d.
BUILT: 1927 by Thornycroft. SINKING: 17th December 1940.
LOCATION: lat 50° 30′ 30″ N. long 01° 32′ 28″ W. (E).
DEPTH: bottom 110′. HEIGHT: 12′. SURVEYS: HMS Scott 1955.
ADDITIONAL: There is a small 6′ scour to the side of the wreck.

Wreck 62. British steamship TERLINGS
DIMENSIONS: 283·5 × 44·4 × 21·6. TONNAGE: 2318 t.g.
SINKING: 21st July 1940.
LOCATION: lat 50° 28′ 15″ N. long 01° 33′ 37″ W. (E).
DEPTH: bottom 109′. HEIGHT: 20′. SURVEYS: HMS Scott 1955.
ADDITIONAL: The bottom is sand and shingle (from the 1955 survey).

Wreck 63. British merchant steamship WESTVILLE
TONNAGE: 3207 t.g. SINKING: 31st December 1917.
LOCATION: lat 50° 35′ 00″ N. long 01° 28′ 00″ W. (E).
DEPTH: bottom 100′. SURVEYS: RN.
ADDITIONAL: Although this wreck is marked as position approximate on the charts, the Royal Navy have now fixed the position.

Wreck 64. Unknown
LOCATION: lat 50° 26′ 58″ N. long 01° 26′ 58″ W. (E).
DEPTH: bottom 104′. HEIGHT: 15′. SURVEYS: HMS Scott 1955
ADDITIONAL: Survey records indicate that this wreck could be a World War Two casualty. The bottom is hard sand and shale.

Wreck 65. Armed British merchant steamship REDESMERE
TONNAGE: 2123 t.g. SINKING: 28th October 1917.

LOCATION: lat 50° 29′ 56″ N. long 01° 21′ 27″ W. (E).
DEPTH: bottom 96′. SURVEYS: HMS Scott.
ADDITIONAL: The bottom is gravel and shell.

Wreck 66. Steamship BRAAT II
TONNAGE: 1834 t.g. SINKING: 7th March 1918.
LOCATION: lat 50° 28′ 50″ N. long 01° 21′ 02″ W. (E).
DEPTH: bottom 105′. HEIGHT: 18′. SURVEYS: HMS Scott 1955.
ADDITIONAL: The bottom is gravel and shell.

Wreck 67. Belgian merchant steamship LONDONIER
TONNAGE: 1870 t.g. SINKING: 13th March 1918.
LOCATION: lat 50° 29′ 58″ N. long 01° 19′ 16″ W. (E).
DEPTH: bottom 95′. HEIGHT: 24′. SURVEYS: HMS Scott.
ADDITIONAL. The bottom is hard sand.

Wreck 68. Armed British merchant steamship ORIFLAMME
DIMENSIONS: 335·7 × 45 × 28·6. TONNAGE: 3764 t.g. 2424 t.n.
BUILT: 1899. CARGO: benzine. SINKING: 25th November 1917.
LOCATION: lat 50° 33′ 23″ N. long 01° 17′ 43″ W. (E).
DEPTH: bottom 100′. SURVEYS: RN.

Wreck 69. Unknown
LOCATION: lat 50° 37′ 46″ N. long 01° 06′ 22″ W. (E).
DEPTH: bottom 45′. HEIGHT: 17′. SURVEYS: RN.
ADDITIONAL: The bottom is of stiff mud and there is a 6′ scour
by the wreck. It is only known that this wreck was sunk in 1918.

Wreck 70. Steamship CAMSWAN
SINKING: 1917. DEPTH: 35′–40′.
LOCATION: lat 50° 38′ 36″ N. long 01° 05′ 25″ W. Or, B & D
160° 1·47 miles from Yarborough Monument.
No other details.

Wreck 71. British merchant steamship HIGHLAND BRIGADE
TONNAGE: 5669 t.g. CARGO: tin ore. SINKING: 7th April 1918.
LOCATION: lat 50° 34′ 50″ N. long 01° 05′ 10″ W. (E).
DEPTH: bottom 50′. SURVEYS: RN; subaqua (salvage).
ADDITIONAL: Although salvage operations have been completed
on this large vessel, it should still be an interesting dive because
the salvage work was on account of the valuable cargo—there
is every possibility that the wreck itself is virtually intact.

Wreck 72. Unknown
LOCATION: lat 50° 34′ 52″ N. long 01° 03′ 15″ W. (E).

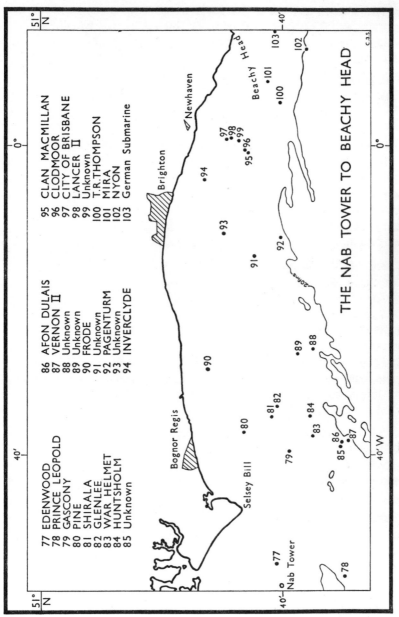

77	EDENWOOD	86	AFON DULAIS	95	CLAN MACMILLAN
78	PRINCE LEOPOLD	87	VERNON II	96	CLODMOOR
79	GASCONY	88	Unknown	97	CITY OF BRISBANE
80	PINE	89	Unknown	98	LANCER II
81	SHIRALA	90	FRODE	99	Unknown
82	GLENLEE	91	Unknown	100	T.R.THOMPSON
83	WAR HELMET	92	PAGENTURM	101	MIRA
84	HUNTSHOLM	93	Unknown	102	NYON
85	Unknown	94	INVERCLYDE	103	German Submarine

THE NAB TOWER TO BEACHY HEAD

Chart 4   The Nab Tower to Beachy Head

29

DEPTH: bottom 60'. SURVEYS: RN 1928.
ADDITIONAL: The fact that this is indeed a wreck and was located during a 1928 RN survey is the only information available.

Wreck 73. Unknown
LOCATION: lat 50° 31' 42" N. long 01° 02' 24" W. or
           lat 50° 31' 57" N. long 01° 02' 48" W.
DEPTH: bottom 90'.
SURVEYS: HMS Dalrymple 1948; HMS Jaguar 1963.
ADDITIONAL: The reason for the two positions is because this wreck was first located in the 1948 survey and charted. Another survey, in 1963, failed to find the wreck in the former position, but found one in the latter. As both surveys gave the wreck as being 28' high it is pretty certain that someone is in error. But one thing is sure; there *is* a wreck at one of these positions.

Wreck 74. Steamship LEON
TONNAGE: 2401 t.g. SINKING: 7th January 1918.
LOCATION: lat 50° 36' 00" N. long 01° 02' 00" W. (A).
SURVEYS: HMS Marvel 1955.
ADDITIONAL: As far as is known this wreck has never been actually identified. The 1955 survey reported a wreck to be in position lat 50° 36' 06" N, long 01° 01' 24" W. or 215°, 4·8 miles from the Nab Tower. It is not known whether the second site might be the Leon—or another wreck—as little time was spent at this site.

Wreck 75. British steamship ELFORD
TONNAGE: 1739 t.g. SINKING: 18th May 1917.
LOCATION: lat 50° 38' 08" N. long 00° 58' 29" W.
DEPTH: bottom 51'.
No other details.

Wreck 76. Steamship CUBA
TONNAGE: 11,420 t.g. SINKING: 6th April 1945.
LOCATION: lat 50° 36' 03" N. long 00° 58' 39" W.
DEPTH: bottom 50'. HEIGHT: 38'.

Wreck 77. British merchant steamship EDENWOOD
TONNAGE: 1167 t.g. SINKING 25th December 1939.
LOCATION: lat 50° 40' 30" N. long 00° 54' 10" W. (E).
DEPTH: bottom 50'–60', least 39'. SURVEYS: RN.

Wreck 78. HMS PRINCE LEOPOLD
TONNAGE: 2938 t.g.   BUILT: 1930.   SINKING: 29th July 1944.
LOCATION: lat 50° 34' 41" N. long 00° 55' 43" W. (E). Or,
B & D from the Nab Tower 171° 5·42 miles.
DEPTH: bottom 60'–65', least 48'.   SURVEYS: RN.
ADDITIONAL: This was an infantry landing ship.

Wreck 79. Steamship GASCONY
DIMENSIONS: 360 × 48 × 21·2.   TONNAGE: 3133 t.g.
SINKING: 6th January 1918.   CARGO: hay, guns and charcoal.
LOCATION: lat 50° 39' 27" N. long 00° 39' 42" W.
DEPTH: bottom 50'–55', least 45'.

Wreck 80. PINE
TONNAGE: 545 t.g.   SINKING: 31st January 1944.
LOCATION: lat 50° 43' 05" N. long 00° 37' 10" W.
DEPTH: bottom 25'.

Wreck 81. British steamship SHIRALA
TONNAGE: 5306 t.g.   SINKING: 2nd July 1918.
LOCATION: lat 50° 40' 55" N. long 00° 35' 10" W. (E).
DEPTH: bottom 30'.   SURVEYS: subaqua (salvage).
ADDITIONAL: Some salvage operations took place between
June–August 1957, but these were of a very light nature.

Wreck 82. British steamship GLENLEE
TONNAGE: 4915 t.g.   SINKING: 9th August 1918.
LOCATION: lat 50° 40' 28" N. long 00° 33' 52" W. (E).
DEPTH: bottom 50'.   SURVEYS: subaqua (salvage).
ADDITIONAL: The extent of the salvage operations is not known.

Wreck 83. British steamship WAR HELMET
TONNAGE: 8184 t.g.   SINKING: 19th April 1918.
LOCATION: lat 50° 37' 26" N. long 00° 37' 30" W. (E).
DEPTH: bottom 80'–85', least 36'.   SURVEYS: RN.
ADDITIONAL: Although the position had been fixed on an earlier
survey, this wreck was searched for on a subsequent survey by
HMS Flinders which could not locate the wreck owing to the
'large number of crab pots in the area'. The War Helmet was
torpedoed by a submarine while in ballast.

Wreck 84. Armed British merchant steamship HUNTSHOLM
DIMENSIONS: 290·7 × 41·2 × 16·9.   TONNAGE: 2073 t.g. 1203 t.n.
BUILT: 1914.   SINKING: 11th June 1917.
LOCATION: lat 50° 37' 45" N. long 00° 35' 00" W. (E).

DEPTH: bottom 82', least 49'. SURVEYS: RN.
ADDITIONAL: Torpedoed by submarine.

Wreck 85. Unknown
LOCATION: lat 50° 35' 08" N. long 00° 38' 54" W. (E).
DEPTH: bottom 85', least 71'. SINKING: 1918. SURVEYS: RN.
ADDITIONAL: It is only known that this vessel sank in 1918.

Wreck 86. British steamship AFON DULAIS
TONNAGE: 988 t.g. SINKING: 20th June 1942.
LOCATION: lat 50° 35' 05" N. long 00° 38' 26" W. (E).
DEPTH: bottom 80', least 66'. SURVEYS: RN.

Wreck 87. VERNON II
SINKING: 29th November 1924.
LOCATION: lat 50° 34' 33" N. long 00° 38' 10" W. (E).
DEPTH: bottom 80'–85', least 66'.
ADDITIONAL: The only other information available is that this was formerly named the MARLBOROUGH.

Wreck 88. Unknown
LOCATION: lat 50° 37' 29" N. long 00° 26' 11" W. (E).
DEPTH: bottom 80'–85', least 66'. SURVEYS: HMS Flinders 1935.
ADDITIONAL: This wreck was first located by HMS Flinders in 1935 in the above position, which has since been confirmed.

Wreck 89. Unknown
LOCATION: lat 50° 38' 42" N. long 00° 27' 00" W. (E).
DEPTH: least 70'. SURVEYS: HMS Gossamer 1962.
ADDITIONAL: This wreck was located during the RN survey, which reported that 'The wreck appears to be about 240' long, lying on its side. According to the sounder reading it has two large masts or two funnels and gives the impression of being well silted up.'

Wreck 90. Norwegian steamship FRODE
TONNAGE: 750 t.g. SINKING: 12th April 1943.
LOCATION: lat 50° 45' 48" N. long 00° 28' 54" W. (E). Or, B & D from Littlehampton East Pier, 313° 2·92 miles.
DEPTH: bottom 30', least 24'. SURVEYS: RN.

Wreck 91. Unknown
LOCATION: lat 50° 42' 14" N. long 00° 14' 15" W. (E).
DEPTH: bottom 65'–70', least 50'. SURVEYS: RN.
ADDITIONAL: It is believed that this vessel sank in 1918.

Wreck 92. British steamship PAGENTURM
TONNAGE: 5000 t.g. SINKING: 16th May 1917.
LOCATION: lat 50° 40' 06" N. long 00° 11' 48" W. (E).
DEPTH: bottom 100' approx. SURVEYS: RN.

Wreck 93. Unknown
LOCATION: lat 50° 44' 46" N. long 00° 11' 14" W. (E).
DEPTH: bottom 55', least 43'. SURVEYS: RN 1963.
ADDITIONAL: The wreck is lying SE by NW and is believed to be a steam trawler. According to the survey the wreck is complete except for the mast, funnel and wheelhouse.

Wreck 94. Trawler INVERCLYDE
TONNAGE: 215 t.g. SINKING: 17th October 1942.
LOCATION: lat 50° 46' 12" N. long 00° 04' 26" W. (E).
DEPTH: bottom 50–55', least 40'. SURVEYS: RN.
ADDITIONAL: The Inverclyde was a requisitioned trawler.

Wreck 95. British steamship CLAN MACMILLAN
TONNAGE: 4525 t.g. SINKING: 23rd March 1917.
LOCATION: lat 50° 42' 50" N. long 00° 01' 00" W. (A).
ADDITIONAL: As far as is known this wreck has never been located although the position should be reasonably accurate. The position given is only two cables distant from Wreck 96.

Wreck 96. British steamship CLODMOOR
TONNAGE: 3753 t.g. SINKING: 3rd May 1917.
LOCATION: lat 50° 43' 00" N. long 00° 00' 30" W. (A).
ADDITIONAL: As with the previous wreck, the Clodmoor has never been located. The position given is only two cables distant from Wreck 95.

Wreck 97. British steamship CITY OF BRISBANE
TONNAGE: 7094 t.g. CARGO: none. SINKING: 13th August 1918.
LOCATION: lat 50° 44' 27" N. long 00° 00' 50" E. (E). Or, B & D from Newhaven Church, 203·5° 3·22 miles.
DEPTH: bottom 66'–70', least 40'. SURVEYS: RN.
ADDITIONAL: An unconfirmed report states that magnetic compass deflection occurs in the vicinity of the wreck—must be worth a try!

Wreck 98. Admiralty trawler LANCER II
TONNAGE: 275 t.g. SINKING: 18th July 1918.
LOCATION: lat 50° 44' 11" N. long 00° 01' 10" E. (E). Or, B & D from Newhaven Church, 198° 3·44 miles.

DEPTH: bottom 70', least 48'. SURVEYS: RN.
ADDITIONAL: Sunk in collision.

Wreck 99. Unknown
LOCATION: lat 50° 43' 30" N. long 00° 00' 40" E. (E).
DEPTH: bottom 30'. SURVEYS: RN.
ADDITIONAL: This wreck went down some time during World War One.

Wreck 100. British merchant steamship T. R. THOMPSON
DIMENSIONS: 360 × 47·2 × 24·6. TONNAGE: 3538 t.g. 2261 t.n.
BUILT: 1897, of steel, by Short Bros. CARGO: 5600 t. iron ore.
SINKING: 29th March 1918.
LOCATION: lat 50° 40' 10" N. long 00° 05' 38" E. (E).
DEPTH: bottom 100'. SURVEYS: RN; subaqua.
ADDITIONAL: The surveys report that the wreck is upright. The wheelhouse structure has collapsed into a hold, and there is a gun on the aft deck facing the bow.

Wreck 101. Tanker MIRA
DIMENSIONS: 340 × 47 × 21. TONNAGE: 3700 t.g. 2397 t.n.
BUILT: 1901, of steel, by C. S. Swan & Hunter. CARGO: fuel oil.
OWNERS: Stevens, Sutton & Stevens.
SINKING: 11th October 1917.
LOCATION: lat 50° 41' 08" N. long 00° 08' 20" E. (E).
DEPTH: bottom 100'. SURVEYS: RN; subaqua.
ADDITIONAL: According to the surveys the Mira is lying on its side, bows pointing S, on a bottom of sand. The 16' (steel) propeller is still intact, the cargo holds are well open and the hull is intact but showing signs of corrosion.

Wreck 102. Swiss motor vessel NYON
TONNAGE: 5364 t.g. CARGO: high grade steel.
SINKING: 16th June 1962.
LOCATION: lat 50° 38' 03" N. long 00° 12' 24" E. (E).
DEPTH: bottom 100–110', least 64'. SURVEYS: RN.
ADDITIONAL: The Nyon was sunk in collision with the Jalazao.

Wreck 103. German submarine
LOCATION: lat 50° 40' 37" N. long 00° 15' 06" E. (E). Or, B & D from Beachy Head Light, 174° 3·4 miles.
DEPTH: bottom 95'. SURVEYS: RN.
ADDITIONAL: This vessel was sunk in the early part of World War Two, but the class and number are not known.

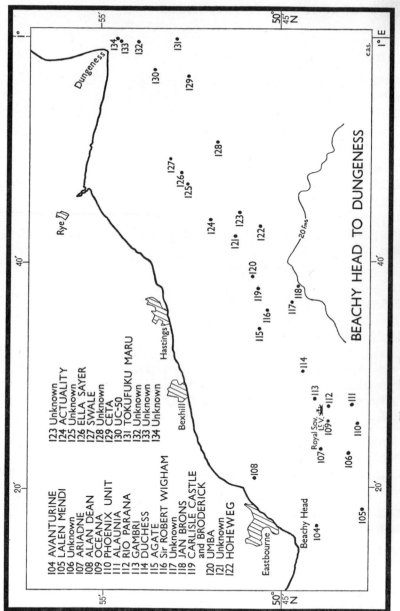

104 AVANTURINE
105 LALEN MENDI
106 Unknown
107 ARIADNE
108 ALAN DEAN
109 PHOENIX UNIT
110 OCEANA
111 ALAUNIA
112 RIO PARANA
113 GAMBRI
114 DUCHESS
115 AGATE
116 Sir ROBERT WIGHAM
117 Unknown
118 JAN BRONS
119 CARLISLE CASTLE
     and BRODERICK
120 UMBA
121 Unknown
122 HOHEWEG

123 Unknown
124 ACTUALITY
125 Unknown
126 ELLA SAYER
127 SWALE
128 Unknown
129 CETA
130 UC-50
131 TOKUFUKU MARU
132 Unknown
133 Unknown
134 Unknown

BEACHY HEAD TO DUNGENESS

Chart 5   Beachy Head to Dungeness

35

Wreck 104. HM trawler AVANTURINE
TONNAGE: 296 t.g. SINKING: 1st December 1943.
LOCATION: lat 50° 43′ 00″ N. long 00° 16′ 30″ E.
DEPTH: bottom 90′.

Wreck 105. Spanish merchant steamship LALEN MENDI
DIMENSIONS: 290 × 42 × 19·5. TONNAGE: 2138 t.g. 1325 t.n.
BUILT: 1896 of steel. CARGO: 3110 t. unscreened coal.
SINKING: 17th November 1917.
LOCATION: lat 50° 40′ 23″ N. long 00° 18′ 00″ E. (E).
DEPTH: bottom 50′. SURVEYS: RN.

Wreck 106. Unknown
LOCATION: lat 50° 41′ 05″ N. long 00° 23′ 00″ E. (E).
DEPTH: bottom 55′. SURVEYS: RN.
ADDITIONAL: It is only known that this wreck was sunk before 1906.

Wreck 107. HMS ARIADNE
TONNAGE: 11,000 t.g. SINKING: 26th July 1917.
LOCATION: lat 50° 42′ 45″ N. long 00° 23′ 21″ E. (E).
DEPTH: bottom 60–75′, least 40′.
SURVEYS: RN; subaqua (salvage).
ADDITIONAL: Ariadne exploded and sank in an explosion caused by mines carried in her after being torpedoed by the German submarine UC65. Salvage has taken place on this wreck and the latest report by the salvage company states that the remains consist mainly of large pieces of plate and scrap.

Wreck 108. Sailing barge ALAN DEAN
SINKING: May 1933.
LOCATION: lat 50° 46′ 30″ N. long 00° 20′ 51″ E.
DEPTH: bottom 26′.

Wreck 109. Steamship OCEANA
OWNERS: P. & O. SINKING: 1912.
LOCATION: lat 50° 42′ 18″ N. long 00° 25′ 50″ E. (E). Or,
B & D from Royal Sovereign Lightvessel, 239° 7·5 cables.
DEPTH: bottom 65′, least 42′. SURVEYS: RN.

Wreck 110. Phoenix Unit number C126
LOCATION: lat 50° 40′ 39″ N. long 00° 24′ 39″ E. (E).
DEPTH: bottom 45′. SINKING: July 1944.

Wreck 111. British steamship ALAUNIA
DIMENSIONS: 520 × 64 × 43.   TONNAGE: 13,405 t.g.
OWNERS: Cunard.   SINKING: 19th October 1916.
LOCATION: lat 50° 41′ 00″ N. long 00° 27′ 15″ E. (E).
DEPTH: bottom 71–75′, least 45′.   SURVEYS: RN.
ADDITIONAL: During the surveys a very heavy swell was noted downtide on the surface of the water. So the wreck should be reasonably easy to locate by this feature.

Wreck 112. British steamship RIO PARANA
TONNAGE: 4015 t.g.   SINKING: 24th February 1915.
LOCATION: lat 50° 42′ 18″ N. long 00° 27′ 04″ E. (E).
DEPTH: bottom 65′, least 37′.   SURVEYS: RN.

Wreck 113. HM trawler GAMBRI
TONNAGE: 274 t.g.   SINKING: 18th January 1918.
LOCATION: lat 50° 43′ 06″ N. long 00° 27′ 51″ E. (E).
DEPTH: bottom 45′.   SURVEYS: RN.

Wreck 114. Steamship DUCHESS
TONNAGE: 336 t.g.   SINKING: World War One.
LOCATION: lat 50° 43′ 48″ N. long 00° 30′ 15″ E. (E).
DEPTH: bottom 60′, least 47′.   SURVEYS: RN.
ADDITIONAL: The Duchess was a railway steamer, previous name DUCHESS OF FIFE.

Wreck 115. HM trawler AGATE
TONNAGE: 248 t.g.   SINKING: 14th March 1918.
LOCATION: lat 50° 46′ 15″ N. long 00° 34′ 03″ E. (E).
DEPTH: bottom 45′.   SURVEYS: RN.

Wreck 116. Target towing vessel SIR ROBERT WIGHAM
SINKING: 3rd December 1956.
LOCATION: lat 50° 45′ 47″ N. long 00° 35′ 48″ E. (E).
DEPTH: bottom 53′, least 46′.   SURVEYS: RN; subaqua (salvage).
ADDITIONAL: Some dispersal operations were carried out in 1959.

Wreck 117. Unknown
LOCATION: lat 50° 44′ 26″ N. long 00° 36′ 27″ E. (E).
DEPTH: bottom 51′.   SURVEYS: RN.
ADDITIONAL: The survey reported that the wreck is in at least two pieces. (Perhaps there is more than one wreck.)

Wreck 118. JAN BRONS
TONNAGE: 400 t.g.   SINKING: 12th October 1945.
LOCATION: lat 50° 44′ 03″ N. long 00° 37′ 51″ E. (E).
DEPTH: least 61′.   SURVEYS: RN.
ADDITIONAL: The bottom, in the immediate area, is very undulating with depths of between 67′ and 94′.

Wreck 119. Steamship BRODERICK
TONNAGE: 4321 t.g.   SINKING: 29th April 1918.
LOCATION: lat 50° 46′ 16″ N. long 00° 37′ 42″ E. (E).
DEPTH: bottom 60′.   SURVEYS: RN; subaqua (salvage).
ADDITIONAL: The Broderick is actually combined with the wreck of the Carlisle Castle (see Wreck 119a below). Some salvage operations were carried out in 1955.

Wreck 119a. Steamship CARLISLE CASTLE
TONNAGE: 4325 t.g.   SINKING: 14th February 1918.
ADDITIONAL: Combined wreck (see Wreck 119 above).

Wreck 120. British merchant steamship UMBA
DIMENSIONS: 291·2 × 41·2 × 18·8.   TONNAGE: 2042 t.g. 1217 t.n.
SINKING: 30th April 1918.
LOCATION: lat 50° 46′ 36″ N. long 00° 38′ 45″ E. (E).
DEPTH: bottom 74′, least 41′.   SURVEYS: Trinity House.
ADDITIONAL: Sunk while in ballast. This was formerly the German vessel UTGARD, which was taken as a prize of war and subsequently torpedoed by a German submarine!

Wreck 121. Unknown
LOCATION: lat 50° 47′ 30″ N. long 00° 42′ 18″ E. (E).
DEPTH: bottom 55′, least 45′.   SURVEYS: HMS Shackleton 1957.
ADDITIONAL: This wreck was first located during the above survey.

Wreck 122. German steamship HOHEWEG
TONNAGE: 1046 t.g.   SINKING: 14th February 1955.
LOCATION: lat 50° 46′ 12″ N. long 00° 43′ 04″ E. (E).
DEPTH: bottom 103′, least 63′.   SURVEYS: RN.
ADDITIONAL: Dispersal operations have been carried out, but only to remove the mast that was a danger to shipping. The bottom is sand and there appears to be no scour to the wreck.

Wreck 123. Unknown
LOCATION: lat 50° 47′ 19″ N. long 00° 44′ 24″ E. (E).

DEPTH: bottom 100', least 76'. SURVEYS: HMS Scott 1955.
ADDITIONAL: This wreck was first located during the above survey. The bottom is sand and there is a 3' scour by the side of the wreck.

Wreck 124. British motor vessel ACTUALITY
DIMENSIONS: 209' (length). CARGO: coal.
SINKING: 27th October 1963.
LOCATION: lat 50° 48' 19" N. long 00° 44' 24" E. (E).
DEPTH: bottom 90', least 46'. SURVEYS: RN.
ADDITIONAL: Sunk in collision with the Betty NS, in poor visibility. Some dispersal operations have been carried out, but only to remove the mast and funnels as they were a shipping danger.

Wreck 125. Unknown
LOCATION: lat 50° 50' 14" N. long 00° 46' 57" E. (E). Or, B & D from Dungeness High Lighthouse 237·5° 8·43 miles. Or, HSF St Leonard's Church Spire 51° 02' to red flashing light at entrance of Rye Harbour 37° 15' to Lydd Church Tower.
DEPTH: bottom 75'–80', least 49'. SURVEYS: RN.
ADDITIONAL: From the survey findings the wreck would appear to be on its side.

Wreck 126. British vessel ELLA SAYER
TONNAGE: 2529 t.g. CARGO: 3900 t. coal.
SINKING: 29th April 1918.
LOCATION: lat 50° 50' 30" N. long 00° 47' 59" E. (E).
DEPTH: bottom 73', least 47'. SURVEYS: RN.
ADDITIONAL: According to the survey findings, the wreck appears to be in two pieces. There is a 9' scour at the side of the wreckage and the bottom is sand.

Wreck 127. SWALE
TONNAGE: 3400 t.g. SINKING: Uncertain, pre-World War Two.
LOCATION: lat 50° 51' 06" N. long 00° 49' 09" E. (E).
DEPTH: bottom 100'. SURVEYS: RN 1944.
ADDITIONAL: This wreck was first located during the 1944 survey. Apart from the name and tonnage, the records of the Hydrographic Department only state 'Very old wreck, sunk before WW2!'

Wreck 128. Unknown
LOCATION: lat 50° 48' 31" N. long 00° 50' 33" E. (E).

DEPTH: bottom 103′, least 80′. SURVEYS: HMS Scott.
ADDITIONAL: This appears to be a large wreck and should be well worth a visit. The survey indicated that the wreck was 300′ long, on a bed of sand, and appeared to be well silted up.

Wreck 129. Dutch motor vessel CETA
DIMENSIONS: 165 × 26 × 9. TONNAGE: 400 t.g.
SINKING: 22nd January 1969.
LOCATION: lat 50° 50′ 03″ N. long 00° 28′ 54″ E. (E).
DEPTH: bottom 95′, least 66′. SURVEYS: RN.
ADDITIONAL: Sunk after collision.

Wreck 130. German submarine UC50
DIMENSIONS: 162–173 × 17. TONNAGE: 400/511 (surface and underwater). SINKING: 4th February 1918.
LOCATION: lat 50° 52′ 00″ N. long 00° 57′ 00″ E. (A).
ADDITIONAL: Sunk by HMS Zubian.

Wreck 131. Steamship TOKUFUKU MARU
SINKING: 25th March 1924.
LOCATION: lat 50° 50′ 44″ N. long 00° 59′ 21″ E. (E).
DEPTH: bottom 116′–120′, least 106′. SURVEYS: RN.

Wreck 132. Unknown
LOCATION: lat 50° 52′ 29″ N. long 00° 59′ 36″ E. (E).
DEPTH: bottom 98′, least 77′. SURVEYS: HMS Scott 1960.
ADDITIONAL: This wreck was first located by HMS Scott.

Wreck 133. Unknown
LOCATION: lat 50° 53′ 56″ N. long 00° 59′ 44″ E. (E).
DEPTH: bottom 94′–104′, least 83′. SURVEYS: HMS Scott 1960.
ADDITIONAL: It appears that this, and Wreck 134, are either two wrecks or one wreck in two pieces as they lie very close together. They were both located by HMS Scott in 1960.

Wreck 134. Unknown
LOCATION: lat 50° 54′ 12″ N. long 00° 59′ 57″ E. (E).
DEPTH: bottom 93′–103′, least 83′. SURVEYS: HMS Scott 1960.
ADDITIONAL: See data for Wreck 133.

Wreck 135. Italian steamship VITTORIA CLAUDIA
DIMENSIONS: 292 × 41 × 18·5. TONNAGE: 2745 t.g.
CARGO: 4000 t. iron ore. SINKING: 16th November 1963.
LOCATION: lat 50° 53′ 43″ N. long 01° 01′ 53″ E. (E). Or, B & D from Dungeness High Light 115·5° 2·52 miles. Or, HSF

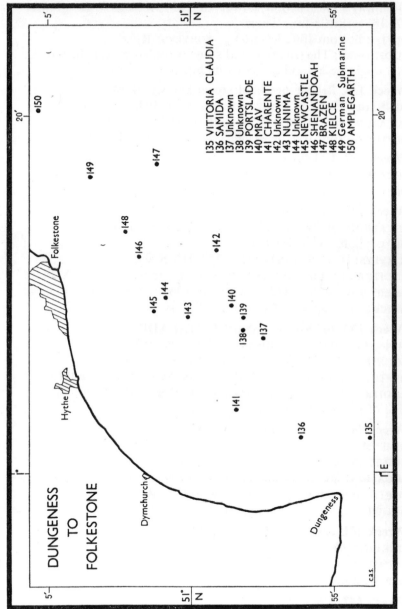

DUNGENESS TO FOLKESTONE

Folkestone

Hythe

Dymchurch

Dungeness

c.a.s.

135 VITTORIA CLAUDIA
136 SAMIDA
137 Unknown
138 Unknown
139 PORTSLADE
140 MRAV
141 CHARENTE
142 Unknown
143 NUNIMA
144 Unknown
145 NEWCASTLE
146 SHENANDOAH
147 BRAZEN
148 KIELCE
149 German Submarine
150 AMPLEGARTH

Chart 6   Dungeness to Folkestone

41

Galloway's Obstruction Tower 26° 28' to Denge Water Tower 27° 18' to Littlestone Tower.
DEPTH: bottom 106', least 63'.   SURVEYS: RN.
ADDITIONAL: The survey noted some turbulence over the wreck; this might be a good guide to its location.

Wreck 136. British merchant steamship SAMIDA
TONNAGE: 7215 t.g.   SINKING: 9th April 1945.
LOCATION: lat 50° 56' 15" N. long 01° 01' 57" E. (E).
DEPTH: bottom 100', least 56'.   SURVEYS: HMS Scott.

Wreck 137. Unknown
LOCATION: lat 50° 57' 36" N. long 01° 07' 51" E. (E).
DEPTH: bottom 82–90', least 55'.   SURVEYS: RN.

Wreck 138. Unknown
LOCATION: lat 50° 58' 20" N. long 01° 07' 36" E. (E).
DEPTH: bottom 90', least 70'.
SURVEYS: HMS Sharpshooter 1949. HMS Scott 1961.
ADDITIONAL: First located during the above survey. A more recent survey by HMS Scott in 1961 reports 'Fairly large wreck; there appears to be a small 3' scour at the side.'

Wreck 139. British steamship PORTSLADE
TONNAGE: 1091 t.g.   SINKING: 20th July 1940.
LOCATION: lat 50° 58' 17" N. long 01° 08' 42" E. (E).
DEPTH: bottom 114', least 64'.   SURVEYS: HMS Scott 1961.
ADDITIONAL: The survey also reported a small 4' scour at the side of the wreck.

Wreck 140. Yugoslavian ship MRAV
DIMENSIONS: 340 × 47 × 20.   TONNAGE: 3890 t.g.
BUILT: 1905.   SINKING: 29th April 1936.
LOCATION: lat 50° 58' 46" N. long 01° 09' 17" E. (E).
DEPTH: bottom 99', least 57'.   SURVEYS: RN.
ADDITIONAL: Sunk in collision.

Wreck 141. Steamship CHARENTE
SINKING: 9th October 1932.
LOCATION: lat 50° 58' 27" N. long 01° 03' 35" E. (E).
DEPTH: bottom 75'–78', least 53'.   SURVEYS: HMS Scott.

Wreck 142. Unknown
LOCATION: lat 50° 59' 07" N. long 01° 12' 42" E. (E).
DEPTH: bottom 104', least 82'.   SURVEYS: HMS Scott 1961.

ADDITIONAL: This wreck was first located during the survey by HMS Scott.

Wreck 143. British steamship NUNIMA
DIMENSIONS: 325 × 47 × 22·4.   TONNAGE: 2938 t.g.
CARGO: iron ore.   SINKING: 5th January 1918.
LOCATION: lat 51° 00′ 06″ N. long 01° 08′ 36″ E. (E).
DEPTH: bottom 80′–90′, least 68′.   SURVEYS: RN 1960.
ADDITIONAL: Sank in collision. Owing to the cargo, it might be possible to locate this wreck by compass deviation—or at least it is worth a try.

Wreck 144. Unknown
LOCATION: lat 51° 00′ 48″ N. long 01° 09′ 47″ E. (E).
DEPTH: bottom 82′, least 53′.   SURVEYS: RN 1960 and 1961.
ADDITIONAL: This wreck was first located during the 1960 survey.

Wreck 145. British merchant steamship NEWCASTLE
TONNAGE: 3403 t.g.   SINKING: 10th October 1915.
LOCATION: lat 51° 01′ 13″ N. long 01° 09′ 00″ E. (E).
DEPTH: bottom 79′, least 35′.   SURVEYS: RN; subaqua (salvage).
ADDITIONAL: This wreck is some 300′ in length. The salvage carried out (in 1969) was of a minor nature.

Wreck 146. Steamship SHENANDOAH
TONNAGE: 3886 t.g.   SINKING: 14th April 1916.
LOCATION: lat 51° 01′ 47″ N. long 01° 12′ 19″ E. (E).
DEPTH: bottom 71′, least 47′.   SURVEYS: Trinity House 1963.
ADDITIONAL: There is a small 2′ scour to the side of the wreck.

Wreck 147. Destroyer HMS BRAZEN
DIMENSIONS: 329 × 32·5 × 12.   TONNAGE: 1360 t.d.
BUILT: 1930 by Palmer & Co.   SINKING: 21st July 1940.
LOCATION: lat 51° 01′ 18″ N. long 01° 17′ 17″ E. (E). Or, HSF Dungeness Light 103° 34′ to Hougham Mast 40° 27′ to Dover Patrol Memorial. A check angle that can be applied is— Hougham Mast 29° 27′ to the right-hand radio mast, or, Metropole Hotel Dome 39° 27′ to Hougham Mast.
DEPTH: bottom 89′, least 58′.   SURVEYS: HMS Enterprise 1966.
ADDITIONAL: This 'B' class destroyer carried arms of four 4·7″ guns, two 2-pounders, five machine guns, eight torpedo tubes. It sank after being bombed.

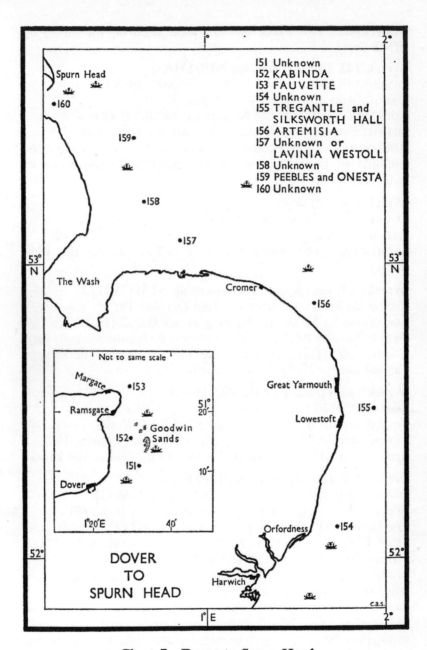

151 Unknown
152 KABINDA
153 FAUVETTE
154 Unknown
155 TREGANTLE and SILKSWORTH HALL
156 ARTEMISIA
157 Unknown or LAVINIA WESTOLL
158 Unknown
159 PEEBLES and ONESTA
160 Unknown

Spurn Head
•160
159•
•158
•157
53° N
The Wash
Cromer•
•156

Not to same scale

Margate
•153
Ramsgate
51° 20'
Goodwin Sands
152•
151•
10'
Dover
1°20'E   40'

Great Yarmouth
155•
Lowestoft

Orfordness
•154
Harwich

52°

DOVER
TO
SPURN HEAD

c.a.s.

1° E

Chart 7   Dover to Spurn Head

44

Wreck 148. Polish steamship KIELCE
TONNAGE: 1896 t.g.   CARGO: bombs, bullets and ammunition.
SINKING: 8th September 1946.
LOCATION: lat 51° 02′ 20″ N. long 01° 13′ 33″ E. (E).
DEPTH: bottom 66′–70′, least 54′.   SURVEYS: Trinity House 1964.
ADDITIONAL: This vessel was on charter to the US Maritime Administration.

Wreck 149. German submarine
LOCATION: lat 51° 03′ 30″ N. long 01° 16′ 36″ E. (E).
DEPTH: bottom 70′, least 55′.   SURVEYS: HMS Scott.
ADDITIONAL: Records indicate that this submarine of unknown class sank in April 1919. There is a small 5′ scour to the side of the wreck.

Wreck 150. Steamship AMPLEGARTH
TONNAGE: 3707 t.g.   SINKING: 10th May 1918.
LOCATION: lat 51° 05′ 20″ N. long 01° 20′ 18″ E. (E). Or, HSF Hougham Mast 54° 13·5′ to Admiralty Pier Light 41° 47′ to Dover Memorial.
DEPTH: bottem 107′, least 61′.   SURVEYS: RN

Wreck 151. Unknown
LOCATION: lat 51° 10′ 57″ N. long 01° 31′ 50″ E. (E). Or, HSF South Foreland Light 33° 21′ to an object called 'Red' (?) 33° 27′ to the Guildford Hotel.
DEPTH: bottom 70′, least 7′.   HEIGHT: 60′.   SURVEYS: RN 1967.
ADDITIONAL: This is a huge wreck and has only recently been found. Its discovery may be due to the pendulum-like swing and movement at the bottom of the South Goodwins Bank which has uncovered it. It might be a World War wreck or something else—we shall never know unless someone investigates. Who knows, in a few years it might have been swallowed up again. It appears to be that of an Island type vessel and is still intact. The wreck produces large swirls and discoloured water particularly on the north-going stream. Large 19′ scour.

Wreck 152. Steamship KABINDA
TONNAGE: 5182 t.g.   SINKING: 10th December 1939.
LOCATION: lat 51° 10′ 03″ N. long 01° 29′ 18″ E. (E). Or, HSF Dover Patrol Memorial 72° 26′ to Guildford Hotel 19° 34′ to Powerhouse Chimney.
DEPTH: bottom 18′–36′, least 5′.   SURVEYS: HMS Ageria.

ADDITIONAL: As can be seen from the depths, the bottom is very undulating. The wreck produces disturbed water on the surface; and there is a large 12' scour westwards of the wreck.

Wreck 153. HMS FAUVETTE
DIMENSIONS: 315 × 43·9 × 18·7. TONNAGE: 2644 t.g.
BUILT: 1912. SINKING: 9th March 1916.
LOCATION: lat 51° 24' 03" N. long 01° 29' 11" E. (E). Or, HSF East Cliff Lodge Flagstaff 33° 58' to Neptune Tower 52° 53' to Margate Sands Beacon. Check angle—North Foreland Lighthouse 19° 08' to Neptune Tower.
DEPTH: bottom 40'–45', least 30'. SURVEYS: RN.
ADDITIONAL: Well away from the Goodwin Sands and only a mile off shore. This vessel struck two mines and sank in four minutes.

Wreck 154. Unknown
LOCATION: lat 52° 06' 21" N. long 01° 44' 20" E. (E). Or, HSF Orfordness Light 56° 14' to Thorpness Roofed Water Tower 37° 10' to Southwold Light.
DEPTH: bottom 70', least 48'. SURVEYS: HMS Scott 1921.
ADDITIONAL: First located during the above survey. Plots right in the middle of a legend on Chart 1408 'numerous wrecks'.

Wreck 155. British steamship TREGANTLE
DIMENSIONS: 323 × 47·1 × 23·7. TONNAGE: 3091 t.g. 1991 t.n.
BUILT: 1903 of steel. CARGO: wheat. SINKING: 22nd April 1916.
LOCATION: lat 52° 30' 40" N. long 01° 52' 11" E. (E). Or, HSF Benacre High Mast 63° 53' to Hockton High Mast 44° 16' to Caister Water Tower.
DEPTH: bottom 97', least 41'. SURVEYS: HMS Sharpshooter.
ADDITIONAL: This is a combined wreck, lying together with Wreck 155a. The survey reported 'Wrecks lie together in 170°–350° direction. Just over 300' in length with a small 2' scour on the north side! Minor dispersal operations have been carried out to remove masts, funnels, etc.'

Wreck 155a. British steamship SILKSWORTH HALL
TONNAGE: 4777 t.g. BUILT: 1907.
SINKING: 10th April 1916. ROUTE: Hull–Philadelphia.
ADDITIONAL: Combined wreck. Data as for Wreck 155.

Wreck 156. British steamship ARTEMISIA
DIMENSIONS: 420 × 54 × 34·3. TONNAGE: 6507 t.g.

BUILT: 1920 by W. Doxford & Sons. SINKING: 14th March 1941.
LOCATION: lat 52° 51′ 41″ N. long 01° 36′ 25″ E. (E).
DEPTH: bottom 70′, least 46′. SURVEYS: HMS Sharpshooter 1950.
ADDITIONAL: This site is only 1·5 miles away from some underwater North Sea gas pipes, so beware—especially if you have permission to do some blasting.

Wreck 157. Steamship LAVINIA WESTHOLL
SINKING: 28th March 1916.
LOCATION: lat 53° 04′ 27″ N. long 00° 51′ 12″ E. (E).
DEPTH: bottom 40′–45′, least 25′. SURVEYS: RN 1920.
ADDITIONAL: It is not certain that this wreck is the Lavinia Westholl. The 1920 survey located a wreck in the last position reported by the Lavinia, and it is presumed that this is it. Investigation might prove otherwise.

Wreck 158. Unknown
LOCATION: lat 53° 12′ 44″ N. long 00° 39′ 58″ E. (E).
DEPTH: bottom 75′, least 30′.
SURVEYS: RN 1962; HMS Echo 1963.
ADDITIONAL: This wreck was first located during the 1962 survey.

Wreck 159. Italian steamship ONESTA
DIMENSIONS: 309 × 42·6 × 16·1. TONNAGE: 2674 t.g.
BUILT: 1896. SINKING: 7th August 1917.
LOCATION: lat 53° 24′ 30″ N. long 00° 36′ 30″ E. (E).
DEPTH: bottom 50–55′, least 39′. SURVEYS: HMS Scott 1962.
ADDITIONAL: This wreck is combined with that of Wreck 159a. The survey reported that the bottom is fairly undulating, and noted that there was a small contact very close NE of this position. This could be part of the combined wreckage, or one of the two wrecks, or even a third, smaller, wreck!

Wreck 159a. Armed British merchant steamship PEEBLES
DIMENSIONS: 380 × 49 × 26·7. TONNAGE: 4284 t.g. 2732 t.n.
BUILT: 1911, of steel, by Northumberland Steamboat Co.
CARGO: coal. SINKING: 13th October 1917.
ADDITIONAL: This wreck is combined with that of Wreck 159. Refer to data of that wreck for other details.

Wreck 160. Unknown
LOCATION: lat 53° 32′ 20″ N. long 00° 08′ 17″ E. (E). Or,

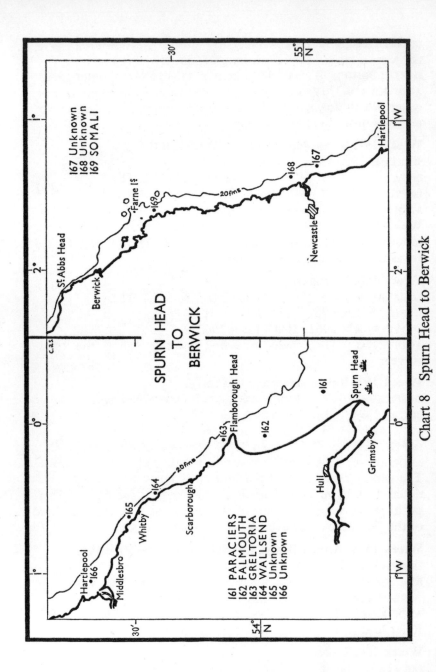

Chart 8　Spurn Head to Berwick

48

HSF Haile Sand Fort 33° 08′ to Bull Sand Fort 62° 37′ to Kilnsea North Tower.
DEPTH: bottom 60′–70′, least 52′. SURVEYS: HMS Enterprise 1968.
ADDITIONAL: The survey report (this was the first time this wreck had been located) states that there is a 7′ scour to the side. And that the bottom is undulating.

Wreck 161. French merchant steamship PARACIERS
DIMENSIONS: 321 × 40·2 × 23·7. TONNAGE: 2542 t.g.
BUILT: 1894. SINKING: 17th September 1917.
LOCATION: lat 53° 45′ 22″ N. long 00° 12′ 36″ E. (E).
DEPTH: bottom 60′–70′, least 47′. SURVEYS: RN 1918, 1949.
ADDITIONAL: Unconfirmed reports suggest that this wreck might be the British merchant steamship WHITEMANTLE, of 1692 t.g., sunk 22nd October 1939. But as the above wreck was first located during the 1918 survey, this is impossible. On the other hand, it could be another 'combined wrecks' site.

Wreck 162. British light cruiser HMS FALMOUTH
DIMENSIONS: 453 × 48·5 × 15·2. TONNAGE: 5250 t.d.
BUILT: 1910 by W. Beardmore. SINKING: 19th August 1916.
LOCATION: lat 53° 59′ 24″ N. long 00° 04′ 48″ W. (E).
DEPTH: bottom 60′, least 42′. SURVEYS: Trinity House 1922.
ADDITIONAL: HMS Falmouth, a Weymouth class cruiser, carried armament of eight 6″ guns, four 3-pounders, and two 21″ torpedo tubes. Some minor dispersal has taken place to remove masts etc, that were a danger to shipping.

Wreck 163. Armed British merchant steamship GRELTORIA
DIMENSIONS: 375 × 51 × 31. TONNAGE: 5143 t.g. 3262 t.n.
BUILT: 1917, of steel, by Northumberland S.B. Co.
CARGO: coal. SINKING: 27th September 1917.
LOCATION: lat 54° 08′ 30″ N. long 00° 05′ 25″ W.
DEPTH: bottom 100′.
ADDITIONAL: This wreck has never been located on a survey, although the position given is presumed accurate. A report has indicated that subaqua divers have located this wreck and that it stands 40′ high, but this is unconfirmed.

Wreck 164. Armed British merchant steamship WALLSEND
DIMENSIONS: 321·2 × 43·2 × 19·5. TONNAGE: 2697 t.g. 1610 t.n.
BUILT: 1917, of steel, by Wood Skinner. CARGO: coal.
OWNERS: Burrett & Co. SINKING: 14th August 1918.

LOCATION: lat 54° 24′ 15″ N. long 00° 28′ 10″ W.
DEPTH: bottom 90′ (estimated).
ADDITIONAL: As no surveys have located this wreck, the position is approximate although there is every reason to presume it correct. The Wallsend was torpedoed.

Wreck 165. Unknown

LOCATION: lat 54° 30′ 48″ N. long 00° 37′ 01″ W. (E). Or, B & D from East Breakwater Light at Whitby, 349° 1·18 miles. Or, a very crude transit, 'A beam line looking down the street on the west cliff of Whitby in line to the steeple of a church in the same street.'
DEPTH: bottom 76′, least 43′.   SURVEYS: 1936.
ADDITIONAL: This wreck was first located by a trawl net in 1936. Although the name is unknown, local information has suggested that this is a steamship named SPARROW. However, no steamship of this name exists at the Hydrographic Office or Lloyd's of London. The charts indicate a wreck at this site as 'P.A.' (position approximate) but this is in error, the fix given above has been verified.

Wreck 166. Unknown

LOCATION: lat 54° 40′ 48″ N. long 01° 01′ 35″ W. (E).
DEPTH: bottom 110′, least 82′.   SURVEYS: HMS Enterprise 1966.
ADDITIONAL: This is a 'brand new' unknown wreck as it was first located during the 1966 survey.

Wreck 167. Unknown

LOCATION: lat 54° 57′ 28″ N. long 01° 17′ 21″ W. (E).
DEPTH: bottom 125′, least 104′.   SURVEYS: HMS Shackleton 1962.
ADDITIONAL: The sea bed here shows numerous small peaks standing 5′–10′ high. This wreck might be the British steamship SUNNIVA (268 × 37·9 × 17·6, of 1913 t.g.), sunk on 19th June 1918 in this area. But this is only conjecture.

Wreck 168. Unknown

LOCATION: lat 55° 02′ 56″ N. long 01° 22′ 12″ W. (E). Or, HSF Souter Lighthouse 30° 42′ to Tynemouth North Breakwater Lighthouse 89° 02′ to St Mary's Lighthouse.
DEPTH: bottom 109′, least 83′.   SURVEYS: HMS Myrmion 1968.
ADDITIONAL: This also is a 'new' wreck only located in 1968. It is a substantial wreck, and there is a very small 1′ scour at the side.

50

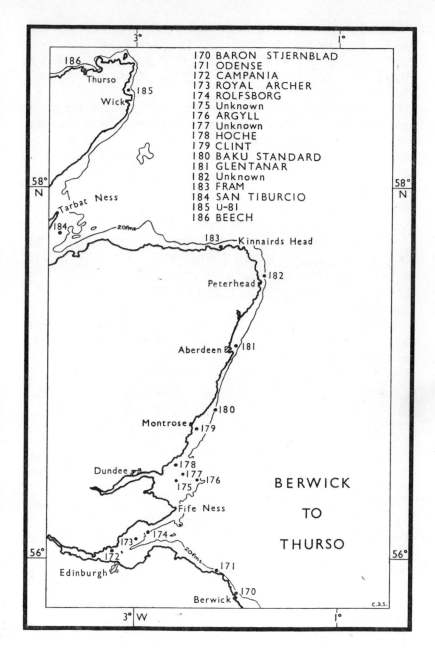

170 BARON STJERNBLAD
171 ODENSE
172 CAMPANIA
173 ROYAL ARCHER
174 ROLFSBORG
175 Unknown
176 ARGYLL
177 Unknown
178 HOCHE
179 CLINT
180 BAKU STANDARD
181 GLENTANAR
182 Unknown
183 FRAM
184 SAN TIBURCIO
185 U-81
186 BEECH

Chart 9   Berwick to Thurso

51

Wreck 169. British merchant steamship SOMALI
TONNAGE: 6809 t.g. SINKING: 27th March 1941.
LOCATION: lat 55° 33′ 56″ N. long 01° 36′ 24″ W. (E). Or,
B & D from Southern Occulting Light of Farne Islands, 147°
3·5 miles.
DEPTH: bottom 71′, least 43′. SURVEYS: RN; subaqua (salvage).
ADDITIONAL: Salvage operations have been carried out, but
only to remove part of the cargo.

Wreck 170. Danish steamship BARON STJERNBLAD
TONNAGE: 991 t.g. SINKING: 23rd April 1917.
LOCATION: lat 55° 50′ 00″ N. long 02° 02′ 00″ W. (A).
DEPTH: bottom 76′.
ADDITIONAL: Although the Baron has never been located, there is
every reason to presume the position given as reasonably correct.

Wreck 171. Danish steamship ODENSE
TONNAGE: 1756 t.g. SINKING: 5th May 1917.
LOCATION: lat 55° 56′ 00″ N. long 02° 12′ 30″ W. (A).
DEPTH: bottom 75′.
ADDITIONAL: Like the previous wreck, this vessel has never been
located although the position given should be reasonably
accurate.

Wreck 172. Aircraft carrier HMS CAMPANIA
DIMENSIONS: 622 × 65. TONNAGE: 1800 t.d.
BUILT: by Fairfields. SINKING: 5th November 1918.
LOCATION: (1) lat 56° 02′ 26″ N. long 03° 13′ 20″ W. (E).
        (2) lat 56° 02′ 20″ N. long 03° 13′ 24″ W. (E). Or,
HSF (1) Oxcars Lighthouse, 89° 10′ to Burntisland Sands
Water Tower 128° 40′ to Inchkeith Lighthouse; (2) same,
92° 0′, 121° 40′.
DEPTH: bottom 80′, least 42′. SURVEYS: RN; subaqua (salvage).
ADDITIONAL: The Campania was a Cunard liner purchased by
the Admiralty and converted to an aircraft carrier capable of
carrying ten planes. It was armed with six 4·7″ guns and one
3″AA gun. Sank after colliding with several ships, including
HMS Royal Oak, resulting in a boiler explosion. The bottom is
muddy. In 1968 this wreck was purchased by Metric Engineering
for salvage.

Wreck 173. British steamship ROYAL ARCHER
TONNAGE: 2266 t.g. SINKING: 24th February 1940.

LOCATION: lat 56° 06′ 26″ N. long 02° 59′ 56″ W. (E).
DEPTH: bottom 70′, least 48′. SURVEYS: RN.

Wreck 174. British steamship ROLFSBORG
TONNAGE: 1825 t.g. SINKING: 13th July 1945.
LOCATION: lat 56° 08′ 17″ N. long 02° 51′ 55″ W. (E).
DEPTH: bottom 120′, least 82′. SURVEYS: RN.
ADDITIONAL: As far as is known, there have been no salvage operations.

Wreck 175. Unknown
LOCATION: lat 56° 25′ 48″ N. long 02° 36′ 22″ W. (E).
DEPTH: bottom 75′, least 63′. SURVEYS: HMS Beagle 1969.
ADDITIONAL: This wreck was first located by HMS Beagle during the 1969 survey.

Wreck 176. Cruiser HMS ARGYLL
DIMENSIONS: 450 × 68·5 × 25·5. TONNAGE: 10,850 t.d.
BUILT: 1905 at Greenock Foundry. ROUTE: Devonport–Scapa.
SINKING: 28th October 1915.
LOCATION: lat 56° 26′ 00″ N. long 02° 23′ 30″ W. (A).
DEPTH: bottom 75′.
ADDITIONAL: The position given should be accurate although the Argyll has never been located. It carried four 7·5″ guns, six 6″ guns, two 12-pounders, twenty 3-pounders, two small machine guns and two torpedo tubes. Sank after running on to the Bell Rock, near Dundee, in heavy weather.

Wreck 177. Unknown
LOCATION: lat 56° 27′ 35″ N. long 02° 32′ 18″ W. (E).
DEPTH: bottom 82′. HEIGHT: 6′. SURVEYS: HMS Beagle 1969.
ADDITIONAL: This wreck was first located during the 1969 survey. Approximately 380′ in length, lying in a 298°–128° direction, it appears to be well buried in the sand. It might be a submarine. The Hydrographic Department would particularly welcome details if any divers examine this one.

Wreck 178. Steamship HOCHE
DIMENSIONS: 277. TONNAGE: 2211 t.g.
SINKING: 29th October 1915.
LOCATION: lat 56° 30′ 16″ N. long 02° 36′ 30″ W. (E).
DEPTH: bottom 70′–80′, least 64′. SURVEYS: HMS Beagle 1969.
ADDITIONAL: The survey reported that the wreck is some 300′ in

length with a small scour. By the readings it is presumed that the wreck is on its side.

Wreck 179. Steamship CLINT
SINKING: 15th March 1927.
LOCATION: lat 56° 42′ 12″ N. long 02° 24′ 30″ W. (E). Or, HSF Scurdieness Lighthouse 19° 05′ to Montrose Steeple 77° 23′ to St Cyrus Church Steeple.
DEPTH: bottom 73′, least 60′. SURVEYS: HMS Shackleton 1955.

Wreck 180. Tanker BAKU STANDARD
DIMENSIONS: 330·6 × 43 × 32. TONNAGE: 3708 t.g.
BUILT: 1903. OWNERS: Associated Oil Carriers.
SINKING: 11th February 1918.
LOCATION: lat 56° 48′ 30″ N. long 02° 12′ 45″ W. (E).
DEPTH: bottom 146′, least 114′. SURVEYS: HMS Ageria 1966.
ADDITIONAL: There is a 6′ scour.

Wreck 181. British steamship GLENTANAR
TONNAGE: 817 t.g. SINKING: 3rd May 1917.
LOCATION: lat 57° 09′ 45″ N. long 02° 01′ 40″ W. (E). Or, HSF Girdleness Lighthouse 50° 56′ to Dance Hall Cupola 25° 43′ to St Machar's Church Spire (north).
DEPTH: bottom 74′–80′, least 66′. SURVEYS: HMS Scott 1958.
ADDITIONAL: The bottom is of sand.

Wreck 182. Unknown
LOCATION: lat 57° 32′ 06″ N. long 01° 44′ 07″ W. (E). Or, HSF Buchannen Lighthouse 23° 40′ to Coastguard Flagstaff 52° 15′ to Triangulation Mark on Beer Hill.
DEPTH: bottom 158′, least 118′. SURVEYS: HMS Scott 1958.
ADDITIONAL: This would appear to be a large wreck. There is a small 2′ scour.

Wreck 183. Swedish steamship FRAYM
DIMENSIONS: 314 × 43 × 20·5. TONNAGE: 2491 t.g.
BUILT: 1897. SINKING: 1st February 1940.
LOCATION: lat 57° 41′ 00″ N. long 02° 11′ 00″ W. (A). Or, B & D (unconfirmed) 259° 2·3 miles, to Pitslago Flagstaff.
DEPTH: bottom 100′ approx.
ADDITIONAL: The Fraym has never been located although the position should be accurate. Torpedoed while at anchor, it broke in two before sinking.

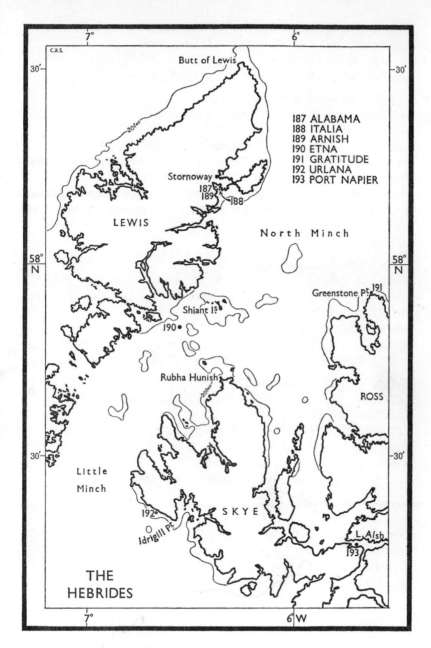

7°

6°

30'

30'

c.a.s.

Butt of Lewis

187 ALABAMA
188 ITALIA
189 ARNISH
190 ETNA
191 GRATITUDE
192 URLANA
193 PORT NAPIER

20 fms

Stornoway

187
189
188

LEWIS

North Minch

58°
N

58°
N

Shiant Is

190

Greenstone Pt.
191

Rubha Hunish

20 fms

ROSS

30'

30'

Little
Minch

192

Idrigill Pt.

SKYE

L. Alsh

193

THE
HEBRIDES

7°

6° W

Chart 10   The Hebrides

55

Wreck 184. British tanker SAN TIBURCIO
TONNAGE: 5995 t.g.　SINKING: 4th May 1940.
LOCATION: lat 57° 46' 33" N. long 03° 45' 20" W. (E).
DEPTH: bottom 80', least 59'.　SURVEYS: RN.

Wreck 185. German destroyer U81
DIMENSIONS: 269 × 24.　TONNAGE: 1188 t.d.
SINKING: 1919.
LOCATION: lat 58° 30' 00" N. long 03° 05' 00" W. (A).
ADDITIONAL: The U81 was scuttled at Scapa Flow, raised, then foundered in Sinclair Bay. A report dated 1937 noted that the wreck had been sold for salvage, but there is no record of salvage operations. It is possible that the salvage attempt was abandoned due to World War Two, and subsequently 'forgotten'.

Wreck 186. HMS BEECH
TONNAGE: 550 t.g.　BUILT: 1929.　SINKING: 22nd June 1941.
LOCATION: lat 58° 36' 39" N. long 03° 32' 00" W. (E). Or, B & D from Littlehead Light 147° 3 cables.
DEPTH: bottom 50'-60', least 27'.　SURVEYS: RN.
ADDITIONAL: Formerly the Lord Dawson, this trawler was requisitioned for World War Two and used as a minesweeper.

Wreck 187. Danish steamship ALABAMA
TONNAGE: 4454 t.g.　ROUTE: Copenhagen–Baltimore USA.
SINKING: 31st December 1904.
LOCATION: lat 58° 11' 50" N. long 06° 23' 02" W. (E).
DEPTH: bottom 26'-47'.　SURVEYS: RN.
ADDITIONAL: Fairly close to shore. The Alabama was driven into Stornoway Harbour for shelter, and sank there.

Wreck 188. ITALIA
SINKING: 1913.
LOCATION: lat 58° 11' 36" N. long 06° 21' 57" W. (E).
DEPTH: bottom 50', least 37'.　SURVEYS: RN.
ADDITIONAL: The bottom comprises sand.

Wreck 189. ARNISH
SINKING: 1923.
LOCATION: lat 58° 11' 22" N. long 06° 22' 47" W. (E).
DEPTH: bottom 34', least 20'.　SURVEYS: RN.
ADDITIONAL: The bottom comprises mud.

Artist's impression of the Bretagne (wreck 32) drawn from general arrangements drawings supplied by the shipbuilders. Artist: John Brown

2　Bell of the Bretagne, recovered by divers of the Bristol Aeroplane Branch of the BSAC. Photo: G. Troote

3 Recovered from the Bretagne by the same divers. A Pelorus? It was hung in a gimbal, probably on the bridge. The base is lead filled to assist stability. Photo: G. Troote

4 Recovered from the Bretagne, also by the same divers. A coat hanger, possibly from the captain's quarters; and a telegraph handle, the wood of which is in very good condition compared to that of other woods found nearby. Photo: G. Troote

5 The Lady Charlotte (wreck 372) aground on Porthellick Point. Photo: Gibson

6 Drawing of the SS Schiller (wreck 362)

7   The MV Mando (wreck 379) on Golden Ball Bar. Photo: Gibson

8   The Earl of Lonsdale (wreck 365). Photo: Gibson

9　The King Cadwallon (wreck 380). Photo: Gibson

10 The Serica (wreck 369). Photo: Gibson

11 The Minnehaha (wreck 370). Photo: Gibson

12   The submarine M2 (wreck 44) shown here after alterations to carry a seaplane. Photo: Imperial War Museum

13 The armed merchant cruiser Otranto (wreck 205). Photo: Imperial War Museum

14 HMS Ariadne (wreck 107). Photo: Imperial War Museum

15 HMS Falmouth (wreck 162). Photo: Imperial War Museum

16 HMS Argyll (wreck 176). Photo: Imperial War Museum

17 HMS Campania (wreck 172) after alterations with twin funnels forward. Photo: Imperial War Museum

18   HMS Campania, sinking. Photo: Imperial War Museum

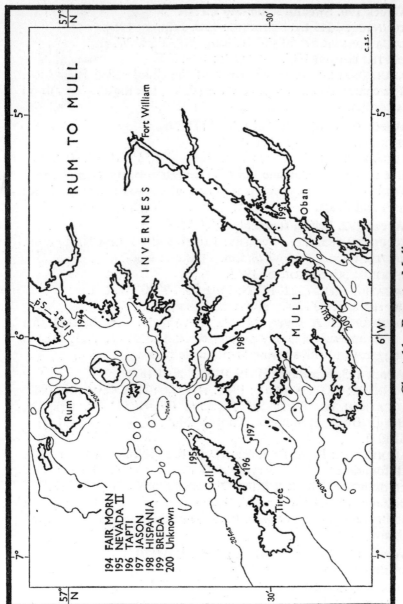

Chart 11   Rum to Mull

57

Wreck 190. Swedish steamship ETNA
TONNAGE: 1645 t.g.   SINKING: 19th January 1954.
LOCATION: lat 57° 50′ 00″ N. long 06° 33′ 24″ W. (E).
DEPTH: bottom 100′.   SURVEYS: RN.
ADDITIONAL: Sank very close E of the shoal called Sgeir Inoe.
The chart indicates the position as (P.A.), but the above position
is correct.

Wreck 191. Fishing vessel GRATITUDE
SINKING: 15th November 1958.
LOCATION: lat 57° 55′ 35″ N. long 05° 36′ 48″ W. (E). Or,
B & D from Greenstone Point Triangulation Mark 356° 1350′.
ADDITIONAL: This wreck is reported to be well tangled up with
nets and floats.

Wreck 192. British steamship URLANA
TONNAGE: 6852 t.g.   OWNERS: British India Steam Navigation.
ROUTE: Buenos Aires–London.   CARGO: wool.
SINKING: 5th September 1943.
LOCATION: lat 57° 21′ 19″ N. long 06° 39′ 20″ W. (E).
DEPTH: least 20′–30′.   SURVEYS: subaqua 1968.
ADDITIONAL: A diver, Mr A. Entwhistle, first located this
wreck and subsequently purchased it. The surrounding area is
dangerous to ships owing to pinnacle rocks.

Wreck 193. Minelayer HMS PORT NAPIER
TONNAGE: 9600 t.g.   BUILT: 1940.   SINKING: 27th November 1940.
LOCATION: lat 57° 15′ 59″ N. long 05° 41′ 12″ W. (E). Or,
B & D from Monument, (stern) 206° 6250 ft, (bows) 211°
6150 ft.
ADDITIONAL: Large for a minelayer, the P.N. lies in Loch Alsh.
It foundered while carrying 600 mines and 4000 rounds of
ammunition. The RN Mine Disposal Team salvaged MOST—
but not all—of the 'cargo'. There is a strong possibility that
some mines/ammo remain. Because of this the RN will not sell
this wreck.

Wreck 194. Motor fishing vessel FAIR MORN
SINKING: 20th August 1969.
LOCATION: lat 56° 58′ 30″ N. long 05° 53′ 30″ W.
DEPTH: bottom 76′.

Wreck 195. Merchant steamship NEVADA II
TONNAGE: 5693 t.g. 8330 t.dw.   BUILT: 1918.

CARGO: general. SINKING: 19th July 1942.
LOCATION: lat 56° 40′ 46″ N. long 06° 31′ 12″ W. (E).
DEPTH: bow dries at lws, stern least 50′. SURVEYS: subaqua.
ADDITIONAL: Divers have reported 'lies on NE side of Rubba
Mor Peninsula parallel to shore, between shore and reef which
is visible at low water springs, 250 feet off shore. Some wave
damage and light salvage, but the hull is still in one piece. The
propeller was removed in 1957.'

Wreck 196. British motor vessel TAPTI
TONNAGE: 669 t.g. SINKING: 17th January 1951.
LOCATION: lat 56° 33′ 14″ (or 40″) N. long 06° 37′ 46″ W.
DEPTH: bottom 70′, least 30′. SURVEYS: subaqua.
ADDITIONAL: The subaqua report stated that the wreck lies
further in towards Soa Island than is suggested by the above
position—but no alternative position was given. The Tapti is
broken into four relatively intact parts except for the engine
room, which appears to have been blown apart by a large
explosion at sinking.

Wreck 197. Torpedo gun boat HMS JASON
DIMENSIONS: 230 × 27 × 12·5. TONNAGE: 810 t.g.
BUILT: 1892. SINKING: 7th April 1917.
LOCATION: lat 56° 33′ 00″ N. long 06° 28′ 00″ W. (A).
DEPTH: bottom 120′.
ADDITIONAL: Although the Jason was a MTB, it was being used
as a fleet minesweeper when it sank after hitting a mine. It
carried two 4·7″ guns, four 3-pounders and three torpedo tubes.

Wreck 198. Swedish steamship HISPANIA
DIMENSIONS: 266·8 × 37·3 × 15·5. TONNAGE: 1340 t.g.
BUILT: 1912. ROUTE: Liverpool–Varberg.
SINKING: 18th December 1954.
LOCATION: lat 56° 34′ 47″ N. long 05° 59′ 13″ W. (E).
DEPTH: least 18′. SURVEYS: HMS Dalrymple 1957.

Wreck 199. Dutch motor vessel BREDA
DIMENSIONS: 402·6 × 58·3 × 34·7. TONNAGE: 6941 t.g.
BUILT: 1921 by New Waterway S.B. CARGO: aeroplanes,
NAAFI goods, tobacco, horses. SINKING: 24th December 1940.
LOCATION: lat 56° 28′ 33″ N. long 05° 25′ 00″ W. (E).
DEPTH: bottom 72′, least 28′. SURVEYS: RN; subaqua.
ADDITIONAL: This is a very popular subaqua dive.

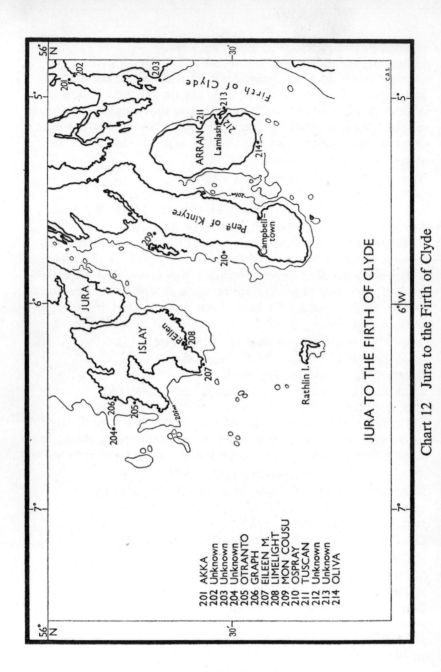

JURA TO THE FIRTH OF CLYDE

201 AKKA
202 Unknown
203 Unknown
204 Unknown
205 OTRANTO
206 GRAPH
207 EILEEN M.
208 LIMELIGHT
209 MON COUSU
210 OSPRAY
211 TUSCAN
212 Unknown
213 Unknown
214 OLIVA

Chart 12   Jura to the Firth of Clyde

Wreck 200. Unknown

LOCATION: lat 56° 19' 32" N. long 05° 55' 33" W. (E).

DEPTH: bottom 45'. SURVEYS: HMS Shackleton 1951.

ADDITIONAL: This wreck was first located during the above survey.

Wreck 201. Swedish motor vessel AKKA

DIMENSIONS: 443 × 56·7 × 26. TONNAGE: 5409 t.g.

BUILT: 1942. SINKING: 9th April 1956.

LOCATION: lat 55° 56' 42" N. long 04° 54' 21" W. (E). Or, B & D from Cantock light 058°, 4·4 cables.

DEPTH: bottom 90'–140', least 60'. SURVEYS: HMS Vidal 1966.

ADDITIONAL: The survey reported that the Akka was lying in one piece, on the edge of the western side of Dunoon Bank. The wreck is nearly upright and on a line 155°–335°, bow pointing S. The bottom is sand, stones, mud and shell. There is no scour. Marked by a small green wreck buoy.

Wreck 202. Unknown

LOCATION: lat 55° 55' 57" N. long 04° 53' 34" W. (E).

DEPTH: bottom 90', least 50'.

SURVEYS: HMS Vidal 1966; subaqua.

ADDITIONAL: This wreck lies in two parts. The northern, larger, portion lies in the position given, the other portion lies southern in position lat 55° 55' 50" N, long 04° 53' 34" W. The subaqua report stated that the northern object consisted of a heavy gantry with a massive toothed wheel, possibly a crane jib or the main drive wheel of a dredger. At the time, the tide was running too fast to examine the hull.

Wreck 203. Unknown

LOCATION: lat 55° 41' 54" N. long 04° 54' 24" W. (A).

DEPTH: 60'.

ADDITIONAL: This is the approximate site of a very old wreck, believed sunk prior to 1790. Presumed to be an old Spanish galleon type vessel, cannon were in fact salvaged from it in 1790, but there is little else known.

Wreck 204. Unknown

LOCATION: lat 55° 49' 18" N. long 06° 36' 26" W. (E).

DEPTH: bottom 150', least 116'. SURVEYS: HMS Hecate 1967.

ADDITIONAL: First located in 1967. This is a substantial wreck and must be that of a large vessel. 800 ft WNW of the above position there is either another piece of the wreck or another, smaller, wreck.

Wreck 205. Armed merchant cruiser OTRANTO
DIMENSIONS: 535·3 × 64 × 38·6. TONNAGE 12,124 t.g.
BUILT: 1909. SINKING: 16th October 1918.
LOCATION: lat 55° 47′ 00″ N. long 06° 29′ 30″ W. (E).
DEPTH: bottom 60′. SURVEYS: RN; subaqua.
ADDITIONAL: Formerly an Orient Steam Navigation Co. liner, the Otranto was requisitioned during World War One and given an armament of four 4·7″ guns. While carrying troops from the USA, it collided with the P. & O. liner Cashmere, drifted ashore and became a total loss. The subaqua report confirmed the position and stated that the wreck was still substantial.

Wreck 206. Submarine GRAPH, P175
DIMENSIONS: 213 × 20·25 × 15·75.
TONNAGE: 769 t. (surface), 871 t. (submerged).
BUILT: 1941, Blohm and Voss. SINKING: 20th March 1944.
LOCATION: lat 55° 48′ 48″ N. long 06° 27′ 38″ W. (A).
ADDITIONAL: Formerly the German submarine class 7C number U570. Captured in 1941 and re-named, it served until lost on tow.

Wreck 207. British tanker EILEEN M.
DIMENSIONS: 136 × 25 × 10. TONNAGE: 323 t.g.
CARGO: oil. SINKING: 12th January 1966.
LOCATION: lat 55° 34′ 42″ N. long 06° 17′ 45″ W.
DEPTH: bottom 50–100′.
ADDITIONAL: The Eileen M. foundered and ran aground under the 400 ft cliffs of the Mull of Oa.

Wreck 208. Motor vessel LIMELIGHT
DIMENSIONS: 89 × 19. TONNAGE: 143 t.g.
BUILT: 1916. ROUTE: to Port Ellen.
CARGO: bricks and bagged lime. OWNERS: Light Shipping.
SINKING: 10th October 1966.
LOCATION: lat 55° 37′ 04″ N. long 06° 11′ 40″ W. (E).
DEPTH: bottom (bow) 30′.
SURVEYS: Northern Lighthouse Board 1967.
ADDITIONAL: The survey reported 'The vessel has broken up and the stern section is still lodged on the rocks at a 45° angle just

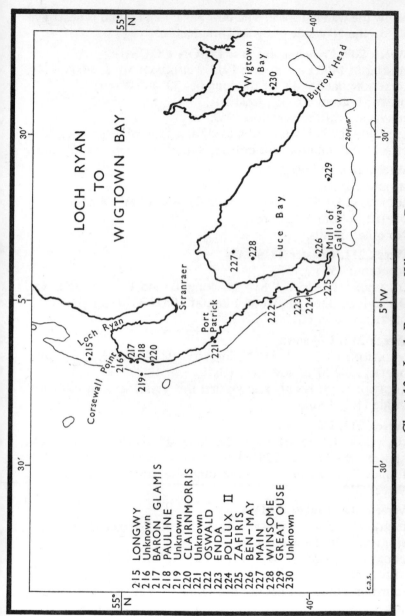

LOCH RYAN
TO
WIGTOWN BAY

215 LONGWY
216 Unknown
217 BARON GLAMIS
218 PAULINE
219 Unknown
220 CLAIRNMORRIS
221 Unknown
222 OSWALD
223 ENDA
224 POLLUX II
225 ZAFIRIS
226 BEN-MAY
227 MAIN
228 WINSOME
229 GREAT OUSE
230 Unknown

Chart 13   Loch Ryan to Wigtown Bay

63

below the water surface. The bow has fallen off and is nearby in 30' on the NW side of Sgeir Thraghaidh.'

Wreck 209. French motor vessel MON COUSU
TONNAGE: 1400 t.g.   BUILT: 1912.   SINKING: 5th January 1944.
LOCATION: lat 55° 42' 38" N. long 05° 39' 49" W. (E).
DEPTH: bottom 30'–35', least 20'.
SURVEYS: HMS Shackleton 1959.
ADDITIONAL: This wreck was used for a little while as a bombing target—but not now. The bottom is sand and there is a 12' scour.

Wreck 210. OSPREY
SINKING: 1935.
LOCATION: lat 55° 31' 00" N. long 05° 45' 00" W. (A).
DEPTH: bottom 60' approx.
No other details.

Wreck 211. Coaster TUSCAN
TONNAGE: 159 t.g.
LOCATION: lat 55° 34' 55" N. long 05° 45' 00" W. (E). Or, B & D from Douglas Hotel Flagstaff, 055° 3850 ft.
DEPTH: bottom 60'.

Wreck 212. Unknown
LOCATION: lat 55° 31' 51" N. long 05° 05' 27" W. (E).
DEPTH: least 51'.   SURVEYS: RN.
ADDITIONAL: It is only known that this vessel sank in 1907, just inside Holy Island.

Wreck 213. Unknown
LOCATION: lat 55° 31' 09·5" N. long 05° 03' 30" W. (A). Or, approx. B & D, 8·5° 225 yd from Pillar Rock Light on Holy Island. This wreck is on the opposite side of the island to Wreck 212.

Wreck 214. Tanker OLIVA
CARGO: benzine.   OWNERS: Anglo Saxon Petroleum Co.
SINKING: 17th September 1927.
LOCATION: lat 55° 25' 45" N. long 05° 13' 24" W. (E).
ADDITIONAL: The Oliva went aground on Bennen Head, and four tugs could not get her off. Eventually it slid back into the sea.

Wreck 215. French steamship LONGWY
DIMENSIONS: 282 × 40·6 × 19·6.   TONNAGE: 2315 t.g.

64

SINKING: 5th November 1917.
LOCATION: lat 55° 03′ 10″ N. long 05° 10′ 30″ W. (E).
DEPTH: bottom 78′–85′, least 48′.   SURVEYS: RN.

Wreck 216. Unknown
LOCATION: lat 55° 00′ 08″ N. long 05° 09′ 57″ W. (E).
DEPTH: bottom 35′.   SURVEYS: subaqua.
ADDITIONAL: Official reports only say that this vessel sank in either 1901 or 1910, with a cargo of whisky. It has been dived on.

Wreck 217. British cargo ship BARON GLAMIS
DIMENSIONS: 301·2 × 40·6 × 16·7.   TONNAGE: 2432 t.g.
BUILT: 1894 by A. Rodger.   ROUTE: Buenos Aires.
SINKING: January 1903.
LOCATION: lat 54° 58′ 32″ N. long 05° 11′ 09″ W.
DEPTH: 50′–70′ approx.
ADDITIONAL: It is rumoured that divers have visited this wreck, but no details have filtered through.

Wreck 218. Coaster PAULINE
LOCATION: lat 54° 58′ 20″ N. long 05° 10′ 59″ W.
DEPTH: bottom 30′–50′.   SURVEYS: subaqua.
ADDITIONAL: This wreck was located by divers and reported at the given position and depth.

Wreck 219. Unknown
LOCATION: lat 54° 58′ 00″ N. long 05° 14′ 00″ W. (A).
ADDITIONAL: It is only known that a vessel did sink about here in World War Two. An unconfirmed subaqua report states that it is 35′ high.

Wreck 220. Clairmorris
LOCATION: lat 54° 56′ 50″ N. long 05° 11′ 08″ W.
ADDITIONAL: Once again, divers located this wreck, in the given position and in 30′–50′ of water.

Wreck 221. Unknown
LOCATION: lat 54° 50′ 30″ N. long 05° 07′ 10″ W.
ADDITIONAL: Located by divers. This is believed to be an immigrant sailing vessel sunk approx. 1890–1900.

Wreck 222. British cargo steamship OSWALD
DIMENSIONS: 258·5 × 37·2 × 18·1.   TONNAGE: 1835 t.g.
BUILT: 1890.   SINKING: 22nd December 1894.

ROUTE: Londonderry–Cardiff.
LOCATION: lat 54° 44′ 30″ N. long 04° 59′ 24″ W.

Wreck 223. Steamship ENDA
TONNAGE: 1500 t.g. SINKING: 25th February 1953.
LOCATION: lat 54° 41′ 25″ N. long 04° 58′ 09″ W.
DEPTH: bottom 50′. SURVEYS: subaqua.
ADDITIONAL: Divers located this wreck, who reported it in the given position and depth. No other details.

Wreck 224. POLLUX II
TONNAGE: 931 t.g. CARGO: tobacco, medical supplies, metal.
SINKING: 26th December 1942.
LOCATION: lat 54° 40′ 27″ N. long 04° 57′ 40″ W. (120′ offshore).
DEPTH: bottom 50′. SURVEYS: subaqua.
ADDITIONAL: On charter to MoW Transport, caught fire, drifted ashore and broke back. The subaqua report (unconfirmed) states that the actual position is 54° 40′ 25″ N, 04° 58′ 02″ W.

Wreck 225. Greek motor vessel ZAFIRIS
TONNAGE: 1600 t.g. approx. CARGO: foodstuffs.
SINKING: 17th December 1965.
LOCATION: 54° 38′ 27″ N. long 05° 55′ 00″ W.
ADDITIONAL: Ran aground and broke in two. It is reported that the wreck is slowly being salvaged, but this is so far unconfirmed.

Wreck 226. BEN-MAY
SINKING: 1938.
LOCATION: lat 54° 39′ 00″ N. long 04° 51′ 30″ W. Or, approx. B & D from Mull of Galloway Light, 350° 9 cables.
DEPTH: bottom 60′, least 45′. SURVEYS: RN.

Wreck 227. British steamship MAIN
TONNAGE: 715 t.g. SINKING: 9th October 1917.
LOCATION: lat 54° 41′ 45″ N. long 04° 50′ 40″ W. (A).
DEPTH: bottom 50′ approx.

Wreck 228. Fishing vessel WINSOME
SINKING: 18th January 1969.
LOCATION: lat 54° 46′ 27″ N. long 04° 52′ 15″ W. Or, B & D from Flagstaff on Balgowan Point, 043° 2·5 miles.
DEPTH: bottom 42′, least 26′. SURVEYS: RN.

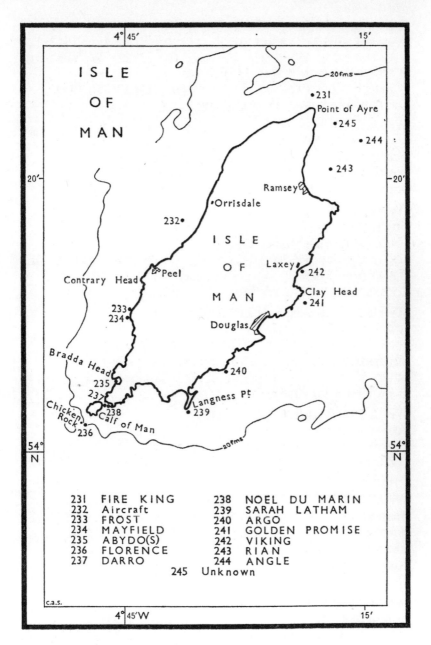

Chart 14 Isle of Man

67

Wreck 229. Dredger GREAT OUSE
TONNAGE: 104 t.g.   BUILT: 1870.   SINKING: 14th June 1942.
LOCATION: lat 54° 38′ 27″ N. long 04° 37′ 29″ W. (E). Or,
B & D from the Big Scar, 116·75° 2·95 miles
DEPTH: bottom 80′, least 53′.   SURVEYS: HMS Vidal 1954.
ADDITIONAL: Lost while on tow by a tug.

Wreck 230. Unknown
LOCATION: lat 54° 44′ 14″ N. long 04° 21′ 04″ W. (E).
DEPTH: bottom 64′.   HEIGHT: 15′.   SURVEYS: subaqua 1968.
ADDITIONAL: This wreck was first located by divers, who reported that it was a fair-sized ship. Wreck 120′ long.

Wreck 231. Steamship FIRE KING
DIMENSIONS: 199·9 × 32·1 × 11·8.   TONNAGE: 758 t.g.
SINKING: 10th December 1939.
LOCATION: lat 54° 26′ 08″ N. long 04° 21′ 54″ W. (E). Or,
B & D from Point of Ayr Lighthouse, 003° 1·2 miles.
ADDITIONAL: Sunk in collision with the Duke of Lancaster.

Wreck 232. Aeroplane. USAF fighter F100
SINKING: 24th August 1969.
LOCATION: lat 54° 16′ 58″ N. long 04° 38′ 06″ W. (E).
ADDITIONAL: USAF divers have removed some instruments, but
otherwise it is intact at a depth of 36′. Classified by local divers
as an interesting dive.

Wreck 233. British steamer FROST
TONNAGE: 209 t.g.   BUILT: 1866.
CARGO: coal.   SINKING: 13th November 1891.
LOCATION: lat 54° 10′ 30″ N. long 04° 44′ 20″ W. (E).
No other details.

Wreck 234. British cargo vessel MAYFIELD
DIMENSIONS: 300 × 39 × 20·5.   TONNAGE: 2632 t.g.
ROUTE: Clyde–Savona.   CARGO: 3300 t. coal.
SINKING: 25th September 1909.
LOCATION: lat 54° 10′ 00″ N. long 04° 44′ 30″ W. (A).
No other details.

Wreck 235. Steamship ABYDO, or ABYDOS
DIMENSIONS: 260 × 31·4 × 21·8.   TONNAGE: 1339 t.g.
BUILT: 1871.   ROUTE: Clyde–Genoa.
CARGO: coal.   SINKING: 26th December 1894.

LOCATION: lat 54° 05′ 15″ N. long 04° 46′ 15″ W. (A).
ADDITIONAL: Foundered off Port Erin with the loss of 19 lives. Strangely, after the loss, bodies, paper and flotsam were found, but not the wreck. At the time of loss the vessel Vito was reported lost at the same place or thereabouts. They might possibly have been in collision.

Wreck 236. British steamship FLORENCE
DIMENSIONS: 149·8 × 22·2 × 10·7.   TONNAGE: 2687 t.g.
CARGO: coal.   ROUTE: Garston–Belfast.
SINKING: 22nd September 1889.
LOCATION: lat 54° 02′ 00″ N. long 04° 50′ 00″ W. (A).
No other details.

Wreck 237. DARRO
TONNAGE: 325 t.g.   BUILT: 1859.   ROUTE: Garston–Larne.
CARGO: coal.   SINKING: 18th July 1901.
LOCATION: lat 54° 03′ 28″ N. long 04° 47′ 45″ W. (A).
ADDITIONAL: The Darro went ashore at The Clets, on the south side of Calf Sound, then slipped back.

Wreck 238. French trawler NOEL DU MARIN
DIMENSIONS: 70·7 × 21·5.   TONNAGE: 117 t.g.
BUILT: 1956.   SINKING: 25th February 1957.
LOCATION: lat 54° 03′ 30″ N. long 04° 47′ 00″ W. (A).
DEPTH: bottom 50′–100′ approx.
ADDITIONAL: This vessel sank in the vicinity of the cliffs at Spanish Head in rough weather.

Wreck 239. Schooner SARAH LATHAM
TONNAGE: 87 t.g.   BUILT: 1903.   CARGO: bricks.
SINKING: 9th July 1948.
LOCATION: lat 54° 03′ 06″ N. long 04° 37′ 27″ W.
DEPTH: bottom 50′–60′ approx.   No other details.

Wreck 240. Steamship ARGO
SINKING: December 1905.
LOCATION: lat 54° 06′ 06″ N. long 04° 32′ 42″ W. (A).
DEPTH: bottom 36′–56′ approx.   No other details.

Wreck 241. Motor fishing vessel GOLDEN PROMISE
TONNAGE: 21 t.g.   BUILT: 1962.   SINKING: 26th September 1966.
LOCATION: lat 54° 11′ 05″ N. long 04° 22′ 45″ W. (E).
DEPTH: bottom 80′–85′.   No other details.

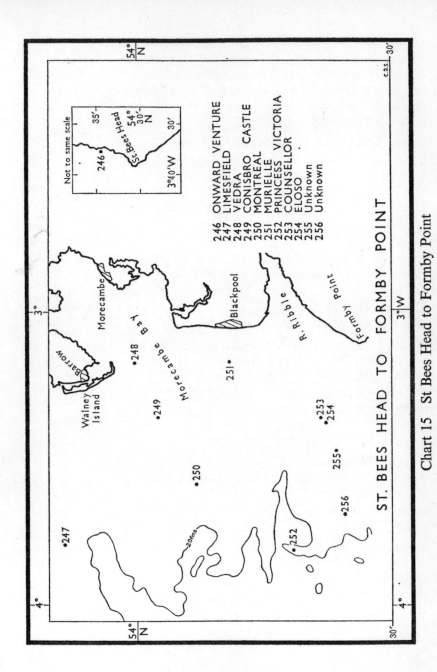

246 ONWARD VENTURE
247 LIMESFIELD
248 VEDRA
249 CONISBRO CASTLE
250 MONTREAL
251 MURIELLE
252 PRINCESS VICTORIA
253 COUNSELLOR
254 ELOSO
255 Unknown
256 Unknown

ST. BEES HEAD TO FORMBY POINT

Chart 15 St Bees Head to Formby Point

Wreck 242. Merchant steamship VIKING
TONNAGE: 262 t.g.   BUILT: 1874.   ROUTE: Swansea.
CARGO: ore.   SINKING: 8th March 1889.
LOCATION: lat 54° 13′ 24″ N. long 04° 23′ 06″ W. (A).
No other details.

Wreck 243. Dutch motor vessel RIAN
DIMENSIONS: 113·4 × 22·1 × 8·3.   TONNAGE 232 t.g.
SINKING: 3rd February 1946.
LOCATION: lat 54° 20′ 44″ N. long 04° 19′ 33″ W. (E).
DEPTH: bottom 45′, least 26′.   SURVEYS: RN.
No other details.

Wreck 244. Steam trawler ANGLE
LOCATION: lat 54° 23′ 00″ N. long 04° 16′ 00″ W. (E). Or,
B & D from Point of Ayr Lighthouse, 117° 3·95 miles.
No other details.

Wreck 245. Unknown
LOCATION: lat 54° 24′ 00″ N. long 04° 19′ 00″ W. (E). Or,
B & D from Point of Ayr Lighthouse, 132° 2 miles.
SURVEYS: HMS Flinders.   No other details.

Wreck 246. Coastal tanker ONWARD VENTURE
DIMENSIONS: 124 × 22 × 9.   TONNAGE: 191 t.g. 97 t.n.
CARGO: diesel oil.   SINKING: 17th July 1969.
LOCATION: lat 54° 34′ 36″ N. long 03° 34′ 48″ W. (E).
DEPTH: bottom 30′–50′.   SURVEYS: HMS Hecla 1969.
ADDITIONAL: Beached and holed after catching fire, the wreck is
slowly sliding down into deeper water.

Wreck 247. Steamship LIMESFIELD
TONNAGE: 427 t.g.   SINKING: 7th February 1918.
LOCATION: lat 54° 09′ 00″ N. long 03° 48′ 00″ W. (A).
No other details.

Wreck 248. Tanker VEDRA
DIMENSIONS: 345 × 44·7 × 22.   TONNAGE: 4057 t.g.
BUILT: 1893.   ROUTE: Sabine (Texas)–Barrow.
CARGO: 6000 t. benzine.   SINKING: 8th December 1914.
LOCATION: lat 54° 00′ 18″ N. long 03° 10′ 38″ W. (E).
DEPTH: bottom 20′.
ADDITIONAL: While stranded on Walmby Island, there was an
explosion which caused the sinking.

71

Wreck 249. CONISBRO CASTLE
SINKING: 13th August 1958.
LOCATION: lat 53° 57′ 23″ N. long 03° 21′ 54″ W. (A).
DEPTH: bottom 60′ approx. No other details.

Wreck 250. Canadian steamship MONTREAL
DIMENSIONS: 469·5 × 56·2 × 31·9. TONNAGE: 8644 t.g.
BUILT: 1900 by Swan & Hunter. CARGO: general.
SINKING: 29–30th January 1918.
LOCATION: lat 53° 53′ 00″ N. long 03° 35′ 00″ W. (A).
DEPTH: bottom 60′–100′ approx.
ADDITIONAL: This vessel was sunk during the night while in Convoy HG47.

Wreck 251. Trawler MURIELLE
TONNAGE: 96 t.g. SINKING: 28th September 1941.
LOCATION: lat 53° 48′ 39″ N. long 03° 10′ 10″ W. (E).
DEPTH: bottom 40′, least 25′. SURVEYS: RN.
ADDITIONAL: Mined, then sank while on tow.

Wreck 252. Steamship PRINCESS VICTORIA
TONNAGE: 1108 t.g. BUILT: 1894, of steel.
CARGO: general. SINKING: March 1915.
LOCATION: lat 53° 41′ 00″ N. long 03° 49′ 00″ W. (A).
DEPTH: bottom 100′ approx.
ADDITIONAL: Sunk in collision with its escort ship.

Wreck 253. British steamship COUNSELLOR
TONNAGE: 5068 t.g. SINKING: 8th March 1940.
LOCATION: lat 53° 37′ 46″ N. long 03° 21′ 50″ W. (E).
DEPTH: bottom 68–70′, least 59′. SURVEYS: HMS Woodlark 1967.
ADDITIONAL: There is a small 2′ scour. The bottom consists of sand, shell and small stones.

Wreck 254. Tanker ELOSO
TONNAGE: 7267 t.g. SINKING: 29th January 1940.
LOCATION: lat 53° 37′ 26″ N. long 03° 23′ 25″ W. (E).
DEPTH: bottom 70′, least 25′–30′.
SURVEYS: HMS Woodlark 1967; subaqua 1968.
ADDITIONAL: The bottom is sand, shell and small stones. 19′ scour. The subaqua report stated 'The length is 250 feet, bows SSE. Cut in half about midships, bow lying upside down, stern on port side. Starboard propeller only has been blasted off. Some salvage. Visibility only good at slack water.'

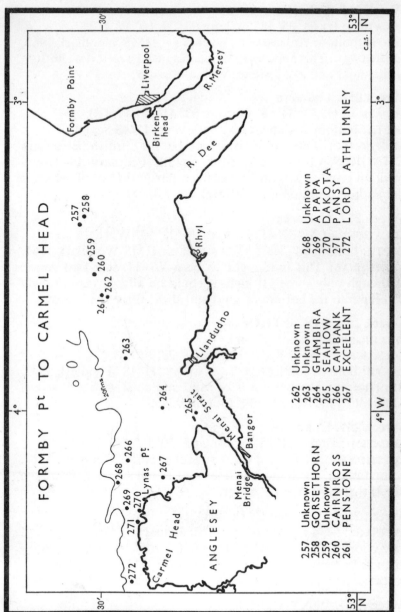

FORMBY Pᵗ TO CARMEL HEAD

Formby Point

Liverpool

R. Mersey

Birken-head

R. Dee

Rhyl

•257
•258

•259
260

261 •
•262

•263

•264

20fms.

•265

Llandudno

Menai Strait

Bangor

Menai Bridge

•266
•268

Lynas Pt.

•267

•269
270

271

•272

Carmel Head

ANGLESEY

257 Unknown
258 GORSETHORN
259 Unknown
260 CAIRNROSS
261 PENSTONE

262 Unknown
263 Unknown
264 GHAMBIRA
265 SEAHOW
266 CAMBANK
267 EXCELLENT

268 Unknown
269 APAPA
270 DAKOTA
271 PANSY
272 LORD ATHLUMNEY

53° N

53° N

3°

3°

4° W

4°

30'

30'

c.a.s.

Chart 16   Formby Point to Carmel Head

73

Wreck 255. Unknown
LOCATION: lat 53° 35′ 58″ N. long 03° 29′ 10″ W. (E).
DEPTH: bottom 70′, least 46′.   SURVEYS: HMS Woodlark 1967.
ADDITIONAL: This appears to be a substantial wreck. The bottom is fine sand and small stones with a 6′ scour.

Wreck 256. Unknown
LOCATION: lat 53° 34′ 58″ N. long 03° 41′ 33″ W. (E).
DEPTH: bottom 104′, least 60′.   SURVEYS: HMS Seagull.
ADDITIONAL: This could possibly be the British steamship CHAGRES, of 5406 t.g., sunk on 9th February 1940 in a position given as 270°, 5·5 miles from Bar Light Vessel, which is the approx. position given above.

Wreck 257. Unknown
LOCATION: lat 53° 32′ 41″ N. long 03° 23′ 40″ W. (E).
DEPTH: bottom 64′, least 53′.   SURVEYS: HMS Woodlark 1961.
ADDITIONAL: This is thought to be a World War Two vessel. Although only some 11′ high, it could be a large vessel slowly sinking into the bottom of sand and shell; there is a 3′ scour.

Wreck 258. GORSETHORN
SINKING: 9th December 1940.
LOCATION: lat 53° 32′ 03″ N. long 03° 22′ 12″ W. (E).
DEPTH: bottom 65′, least 53′.   SURVEYS: HMS Woodlark 1953.
ADDITIONAL: The bottom is of sand and shell with a 5′ scour. Difficult to locate as the bottom undulates.

Wreck 259. Unknown
LOCATION: lat 53° 31′ 16″ N. long 03° 30′ 48″ W. (E).
DEPTH: bottom 88′, least 68′.   SURVEYS: HMS Woodlark 1967.
ADDITIONAL: The bottom is fine sand, small stones and broken shell; there is a small 2′ scour.

Wreck 260. Steamship CAIRNROSS
TONNAGE: 5494 t.g.   SINKING: 17th January 1948.
LOCATION: lat 53° 30′ 54″ N. long 03° 33′ 06″ W. (E).
DEPTH: bottom 86′, least 86′.   SURVEYS: HMS Woodlark.
ADDITIONAL: There is a 6′ scour.

Wreck 261. PENSTONE
TONNAGE: 267 t.g.   SINKING: 31st July 1948.
LOCATION: lat 53° 29′ 52″ N. long 03° 37′ 29″ W. (E).

74

DEPTH: bottom 96', least 84'. SURVEYS: HMS Woodlark.
ADDITIONAL: The bottom consists of sand and small stones.

Wreck 262. Unknown
LOCATION: lat 53° 29' 36" N. long 03° 38' 00" W. (E).
DEPTH: bottom 95', least 70'. SURVEYS: HMS Woodlark 1967.
ADDITIONAL: This seems to be a substantial wreck. The bottom
consists of sand and small stones; there is a small 2' scour.

Wreck 263. Unknown
LOCATION: lat 53° 27' 10" N. long 03° 49' 55" W. (E).
DEPTH: bottom 85'. SURVEYS: HMS Eglet 1939.
ADDITIONAL: It is believed this vessel sank in 1930, but this is
unconfirmed.

Wreck 264. GHAMBIRA
SINKING: 15th October 1943.
LOCATION: lat 53° 23' 00" N. long 03° 59' 38" W. (E).
DEPTH: bottom 60', least 43'. SURVEYS: RN.

Wreck 265. SEAHOW
SINKING: 19th May 1969.
LOCATION: lat 53° 19' 03" N. long 04° 00' 03" W.
ADDITIONAL: The Seahow is believed to have been an iron self-
propelled barge some 160' long which sank in rough weather.
The bottom in this area averages 83'.

Wreck 266. British merchant steamship CAMBANK
DIMENSIONS: 323 × 47·1 × 25. BUILT: 1899.
TONNAGE: 3112 t.g. CARGO: copper and sulphur ore.
SINKING: 20th February 1915.
LOCATION: lat 53° 26' 40" N. long 04° 09' 54" W. (E).
DEPTH: bottom 110', least 83'.
SURVEYS: RN; subaqua (salvage).
ADDITIONAL: Some salvage has been carried out on the cargo
only, and it is assumed that only three-quarters of the cargo was
recovered.

Wreck 267. Ketch EXCELLENT
DIMENSIONS: 135 × 23· 3 × 10·5. TONNAGE: 351 t.g.
BUILT: 1920. SINKING: 1926.
LOCATION: lat 53° 22' 30" N. long 04° 12' 45" W.
DEPTH: bottom 55'.
ADDITIONAL: Sunk in collision with HMS Folkestone.

Wreck 268. Unknown
LOCATION: lat 53° 28′ 13″ N. long 04° 14′ 06″ W. (E).
DEPTH: bottom 112′.   SURVEYS: HMS Seagull 1946.
ADDITIONAL: This is presumed to be a World War Two wreck.

Wreck 269. Armed merchant steamship APAPA
DIMENSIONS: 425·7 × 57·3 × 31·3.   TONNAGE: 7832 t.g.
ROUTE: returning from W. Africa.
SINKING: 28th November 1917.
LOCATION: lat 53° 26′ 45″ N. long 04° 18′ 50″ W. (E).
DEPTH: bottom 112′.   SURVEYS: Trinity House 1931.
ADDITIONAL: This substantial wreck, as far as is known, has never been dived on or visited by survey ships since it was first located in 1931.

Wreck 270. Steamship DAKOTA
DIMENSIONS: 400·6 × 43·3 × 32·7.   TONNAGE: 4332 t.g. 2482 t.n.
BUILT: 1874.   ROUTE: Liverpool–New York.
CARGO: earthenware.   SINKING: 9th May 1877.
LOCATION: lat 53° 25′ 11″ N. long 04° 20′ 24″ W. (E).
DEPTH: bottom (bows) 30′, (stern) 70′.   SURVEYS: subaqua.
ADDITIONAL: Most of the cargo was salvaged. A divers' report states 'Wreck is still together, in good condition, but gradually collapsing' (this was in 1969). Iron screwsteamer.

Wreck 271. Paddle steamer PANSY
DIMENSIONS: 160 × 27·1 × 9·9.   TONNAGE: 333 t.g.
BUILT: 1896.
LOCATION: lat 53° 25′ 24″ N. long 04° 21′ 54″ W. (E).
DEPTH: bottom 50′–60′.   SURVEYS: subaqua.
ADDITIONAL: This wreck was first located by divers in 1968. The report states 'Fairly well broken up on sea bed. Parts of huge paddle wheels and isolated sections 15′ high, bed steep and shelving.' Unconfirmed reports suggest that Pansy sank in a NE gale in 1915, on route to the South Coast.

Wreck 272. Steamer LORD ATHLUMNEY
SINKING: 4th June 1887.
LOCATION: lat 53° 26′ 10″ N. long 04° 32′ 33″ W.
DEPTH: 60′–70′ approx.
ADDITIONAL: Wrecked on Coal Rock, which is visible at low water springs.

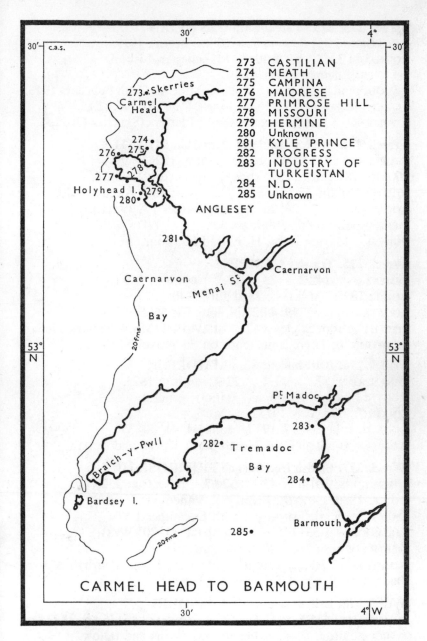

273 CASTILIAN
274 MEATH
275 CAMPINA
276 MAIORESE
277 PRIMROSE HILL
278 MISSOURI
279 HERMINE
280 Unknown
281 KYLE PRINCE
282 PROGRESS
283 INDUSTRY OF
    TURKEISTAN
284 N.D.
285 Unknown

CARMEL HEAD TO BARMOUTH

Chart 17 Carmel Head to Barmouth

Wreck 273. British steamship CASTILIAN
DIMENSIONS: 331·3 × 46·8 × 23·2.   BUILT: 1919.
TONNAGE: 3067 t.g.   ROUTE: Manchester–Lisbon.
OWNERS: Elleman Lines.
CARGO: mail and copper sulphate.   SINKING: 12th February 1943.
LOCATION: lat 53° 25' 21" N. long 04° 36' 30" W. (E).
ADDITIONAL: Ran ashore on the E. Platters (Skerries Group).

Wreck 274. British merchant steamship MEATH
DIMENSIONS: 321 × 40 × 16.   BUILT: 1929.
CARGO: 781 cattle, 1008 sheep.   TONNAGE: 1598 t.g.
ROUTE: Dublin–Birkenhead.   SINKING: 16th August 1940.
LOCATION: lat 53° 20' 24" N. long 04° 36' 17" W. (E).
DEPTH: bottom 45'–50', least 30'.
SURVEYS: Marine Dept, Holyhead Harbour.

Wreck 275. Trawler CAMPINA
DIMENSIONS: 142·2 × 23 × 13.   TONNAGE: 289 t.g.
BUILT: 1896.   SINKING: 23rd July 1940.
LOCATION: lat 53° 19' 49·2" N. long 04° 36' 56·6" W. (E).
DEPTH: bottom 52', least 42'.   SURVEYS: HMS Woodlark 1968.
ADDITIONAL: There is no scour on the gravel bottom.

Wreck 276. British steamship MAIORESE
DIMENSIONS: 272 × 33·4 × 22·9.   BUILT: 1875.
ROUTE: Liverpool–Genoa.   CARGO: general.
SINKING: 23rd May 1913.
LOCATION: lat 53° 19' 19" N. long 04° 41' 00" W.
ADDITIONAL: Struck the North Stack Rocks and sank.

Wreck 277. British iron barque PRIMROSE HILL
DIMENSIONS: 301·6 × 42·1 × 24·7.   TONNAGE: 2520 t.g.
BUILT: 1886.   ROUTE: Liverpool–Vancouver.
CARGO: general.   SINKING: 28th December 1900.
LOCATION: lat 53° 17' 26" N. long 04° 41' 00" W. (E).
DEPTH: bottom 30'.   SURVEYS: subaqua.
ADDITIONAL: Ran aground on Penrhos Rock, Penrhyn Mawr.
Badly broken up. A four-masted barque.

Wreck 278. British steamship MISSOURI
DIMENSIONS: 425·6 × 43·6 × 27·9.   TONNAGE: 5146 t.g. 3332 t.n.
CARGO: cotton, flour, palm oil, provisions and tallow.
SINKING: 1st March 1886.

LOCATION: lat 53° 17' 00" N. long 04° 39' 25" W. (E).
DEPTH: bottom 30'–40', least 15'. SURVEYS: subaqua.
ADDITIONAL: One of the most popular dives in the area. Part of the cargo was recovered. The wreck is broken up, but all the steering gear is standing clear of a rocky bottom. Missouri was a four-masted iron screw steamer.

Wreck 279. British iron barque HERMINE
DIMENSIONS: 159·7 × 27·4 × 18. TONNAGE: 538 t.g.
ROUTE: Scepe–Liverpool. CARGO: sugar.
SINKING: 16th June 1890.
LOCATION: lat 53° 15' 45" N. long 04° 37' 08" W. (E).
DEPTH: bottom 30'–40'. SURVEYS: subaqua.
ADDITIONAL: Divers located this wreck, which is well broken up, but worth a visit.

Wreck 280. Unknown
LOCATION: lat 53° 15' 12" N. long 04° 37' 54" W. (E).
ADDITIONAL: This wreck lies at the bottom of Maen Piscar Rock. It is quite old, and well broken up. There are traces of lead and other metals on the sea bed round the wreck. One underwater detective has suggested that this might be the steamship HAVSO.

Wreck 281. British steamship KYLE PRINCE
DIMENSIONS: 155 × 23·9 × 9·9. TONNAGE: 409 t.g. 163 t.n.
ROUTE: Barry–Liverpool. CARGO: cement.
SINKING: 8th October 1938.
LOCATION: lat 53° 11' 26" N. long 04° 30' 18" W. (E).
DEPTH: bottom 20'–30'. SURVEYS: subaqua.
ADDITIONAL: Wrecked after being abandoned in heavy weather with engine trouble. Well broken up but still a good dive. The bottom is rocky, and the many pinnacles of rock make the area dangerous for shipping.

Wreck 282. PROGRESS
SINKING: 1928 approx.
LOCATION: lat 52° 51' 16" N. long 04° 24' 10" W. (E). Or, B & D from Gimlett Rock, 005° 1·7 miles (approx.).
DEPTH: least 26'. SURVEYS: HMS Medusa 1964.
ADDITIONAL: Although the position given is correct, the 1964 survey could not re-locate the wreck owing to the undulating bottom.

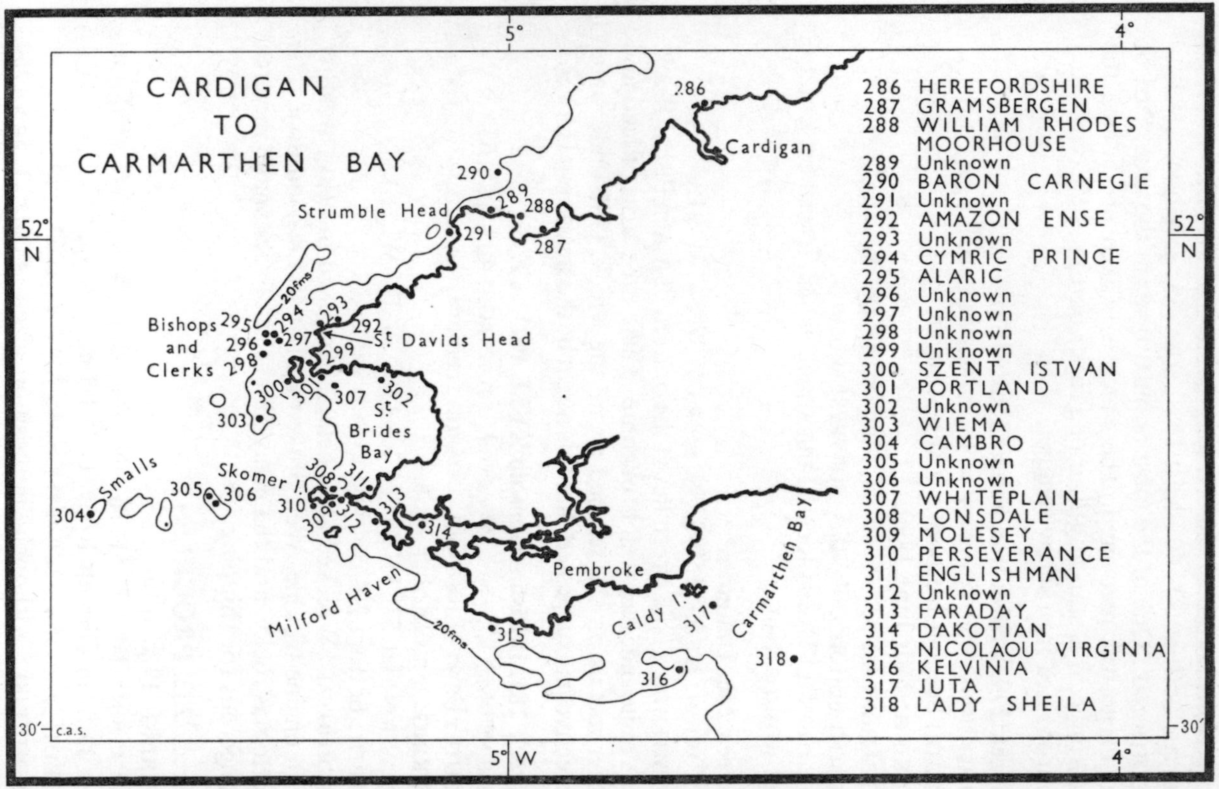

CARDIGAN
TO
CARMARTHEN BAY
286 HEREFORDSHIRE
287 GRAMSBERGEN
288 WILLIAM RHODES MOORHOUSE
289 Unknown
290 BARON CARNEGIE
291 Unknown
292 AMAZON ENSE
293 Unknown
294 CYMRIC PRINCE
295 ALARIC
296 Unknown
297 Unknown
298 Unknown
299 Unknown
300 SZENT ISTVAN
301 PORTLAND
302 Unknown
303 WIEMA
304 CAMBRO
305 Unknown
306 Unknown
307 WHITEPLAIN
308 LONSDALE
309 MOLESEY
310 PERSEVERANCE
311 ENGLISHMAN
312 Unknown
313 FARADAY
314 DAKOTIAN
315 NICOLAOU VIRGINIA
316 KELVINIA
317 JUTA
318 LADY SHEILA
Cardigan
Strumble Head
St Davids Head
Bishops and Clerks
St Brides Bay
Skomer I.
Smalls
Milford Haven
Pembroke
Caldy I.
Carmarthen Bay
20fms
52° N
5° W
4°
30′
c.a.s.

Chart 18 Cardigan to Carmarthen Bay

Wreck 283. Sailing vessel INDUSTRY OF TURKESTAN
SINKING: 1950.
LOCATION: lat 52° 53′ 16″ N. long 04° 19′ 38″ W.
DEPTH: bottom 30′ approx. No other details.

Wreck 284. Schooner N.D.
SINKING: 1924.
LOCATION: lat 52° 47′ 24″ N. long 04° 19′ 40″ W. (E).
DEPTH: 15′–30′ approx. No other details.

Wreck 285. Unknown
LOCATION: lat 52° 42′ 21″ N. long 04° 19′ 28″ W. (E).
SURVEYS: HMS Medusa 1965.
ADDITIONAL: Lying at the end of a sandbar called The Causeway, this wreck is believed to have sunk in 1890. The wreck consists of hull framing, boilers, and much small sundry wreckage spread out some 20′. The tides are strong and this is a slack water dive only. Parts of The Causeway dry at low water. Unconfirmed reports say that there is also wreckage 1 mile S of this position.

Wreck 286. British steamship HEREFORDSHIRE
TONNAGE: 4504 t.g. SINKING: 15th March 1934.
LOCATION: lat 52° 17′ 57″ N. long 04° 41′ 05″ W. (E).
DEPTH: bottom 60′–70′. SURVEYS: subaqua.
ADDITIONAL: This wreck might have been purchased by Llanelly Subaqua Club.

Wreck 287. Coaster GRAMSBERGEN
TONNAGE: 498 t.g. SINKING: November 1955.
LOCATION: lat 52° 08′ 50″ N. long 04° 56′ 03″ W. (E).
DEPTH: bottom 40′. HEIGHT: 18′. SURVEYS: subaqua.
No other details.

Wreck 288. Motor fishing vessel WILLIAM RHODES MOORHOUSE
DIMENSIONS: 93 × 22 × 11. TONNAGE: 112 t.g.
SINKING: 14th April 1968.
LOCATION: lat 52° 01′ 38″ N. long 04° 58′ 29″ W. (E).
DEPTH: bottom 75′–80′, least 63′. SURVEYS: Trinity House.

Wreck 289. Unknown
LOCATION: lat 52° 01′ 30″ N. long 05° 01′ 00″ W. (A).
ADDITIONAL: First located by divers on the east side of Strumble

Head beneath a hamlet called Trefasser. The wreck is 10' high and the wreckage extends from the cliff for 200' seawards. It is covered by weed and boulders and is difficult to locate, but it must have been a large vessel.

Wreck 290. British merchant steamship BARON CARNEGIE
DIMENSIONS: 336·3 × 48·5 × 22·2. TONNAGE: 3178 t.g. 5500 t.dw.
OWNERS: Kelvin Shipping. BUILT: 1925.
ROUTE: in convoy off Mumbles. SINKING: 11th June 1941.
LOCATION: lat 52° 04' 12" N. long 05° 01' 10" W. (E).
DEPTH: bottom 132'. HEIGHT: 30'–35'. SURVEYS: RN.

Wreck 291. Unknown
LOCATION: lat 52° 00' 57" N. long. 05° 05' 30" W.
DEPTH: bottom 100'–120'. SURVEYS: RN.
ADDITIONAL: This is believed to have been a vessel of at least 1000 t.g. No other details.

Wreck 292. Coaster AMAZON ENSE
DIMENSIONS: 286·7 × 34·7 × 24. TONNAGE: 1865 t.g.
BUILT: 1879 of iron. SINKING: 16th April 1881.
LOCATION: lat 51° 54' 46" N. long 05° 16' 33" W.
DEPTH: bottom 30'. SURVEYS: subaqua 1968.
ADDITIONAL: First located by divers in 1968, who reported that the wreckage stands 10' high. The bottom is of large boulders and the wreckage is strewn around. Propeller (iron) and stern end are complete. Some salvage has taken place.

Wreck 293. Unknown
LOCATION: lat 51° 54' 36" N. long 05° 17' 54" W. (E).
DEPTH: bottom 50' approx. SURVEYS: subaqua.
ADDITIONAL: First located by divers in 1969. This might be the British cargo steamship GLENISLA, built in 1883 of iron, dimensions 265 × 36·2 × 17, tonnage 1559 gross, which struck a rock near St David's Head on 28th February 1886.

Wreck 294. CYMRIC PRINCE
DIMENSIONS: 340·3 × 47·2 × 26·1. TONNAGE: 3445 t.g.
BUILT: 1901. CARGO: iron ore. SINKING: 24th February 1917.
LOCATION: lat 51° 54' 10" N. long 05° 22' 52" W. (E).
DEPTH: bottom 50'–60' approx.
ADDITIONAL: Formerly the KYLENESS.

Wreck 295. ALARIC
LOCATION: lat 51° 54′ 13.5″ N. long 05° 22′ 59·5″ W.
DEPTH: bottom 50′. SURVEYS: subaqua 1968.
ADDITIONAL: First located by divers in 1968, the remains look like that of a steel hulled sailing vessel (said by local fishermen to be the Alaric). There is wreckage in a position 211·5° 400 ft from the above position—this may be part of the Alaric, or another wreck.

Wreck 296. Unknown
LOCATION: lat 51° 53′ 55″ N. long 05° 23′ 42″ W.
SURVEYS: subaqua 1967.
ADDITIONAL: It is only known that this wreck was located by divers in 1967. It may be a danger to fishermen.

Wreck 297. Unknown
LOCATION: lat 51° 53′ 57·5″ N. long 05° 21′ 18″ W. (E).
ADDITIONAL: First located by divers on the NW side of Carreg Tral. It appears to be a large vessel, but bad weather precluded a close investigation.

Wreck 298. Unknown
LOCATION: lat 51° 52′ 53″ N. long 05° 23′ 44″ W. (E).
SURVEYS: subaqua 1968.
ADDITIONAL: This wreck was located by divers slightly NW of Maen Rock, but no report has been submitted.

Wreck 299. Unknown
LOCATION: lat 51° 52′ 16·5″ N. long 05° 19′ 12″ W. (E).
DEPTH: bottom 30′–50′. SURVEYS: subaqua.
ADDITIONAL: This vessel obviously struck Horse Rock. The divers have not submitted a report, but the 'detectives' in the Hydrographic Department say this could be the British steamship COUNT D'ASPREMONT, built in 1874 of iron, 452 t.g., dimensions 162·5 × 23·2 × 14. This vessel sank on 15th December 1903 while on route Dublin–Newport.

Wreck 300. Steamship SZENT ISTVAN
DIMENSIONS: 285 × 38·2 × 23·2. TONNAGE: 2215 t.g.
SINKING: 28th September 1909.
LOCATION: lat 51° 51′ 24″ N. long 05° 20′ 55″ W. (E).
DEPTH: bottom 35′–45′, least 13′. SURVEYS: subaqua 1968.
ADDITIONAL: Located by divers. The vessel's back is broken, and

the propeller is missing—presumably as the result of salvage. The bottom consists of small boulders.

Wreck 301. Wooden auxiliary vessel PORTLAND
TONNAGE: 54 t.g. 34 t.n.   BUILT: 1868 in Britain.
ROUTE: Porth Gain–Pembroke. CARGO: stones.
SINKING: 9th December 1927.
LOCATION: lat 51° 51′ 45″ N. long 05° 18′ 02″ W. (E).
SURVEYS: subaqua.
ADDITIONAL: Located by divers. The last subaqua report (1968) stated that the wreck was still fairly well intact, and the cargo can still be seen in the wreck. It is said that a Mr A. J. John owned the vessel at the time of sinking.

Wreck 302. Unknown
LOCATION: lat 51° 51′ 27″ N. long 05° 12′ 20″ W. (E).
DEPTH: bottom 50′.   SURVEYS: subaqua.
ADDITIONAL: This wreck was first located when divers investigated a snagged fishing net in 1969. Apparently the vessel could have been larger than a trawler, and the divers recovered a compass with a Patent date 1875 on it. Local knowledge suggests that the wreck is only 30 years old.

Wreck 303. Dutch motor vessel WIEMA
SINKING: 10th December 1961.
LOCATION: lat 51° 49′ 02″ N. long 05° 23′ 54″ W. (E). Or, B & D from South Bishop Light, 168° 2·18 miles.
DEPTH: bottom 105′.   SURVEYS: RN.
ADDITIONAL: The cargo shifted in a gale.

Wreck 304. British cargo ship CAMBRO
DIMENSIONS: 282·3 × 40 × 19·3.   TONNAGE: 1918 t.g.
BUILT: 1906.   ROUTE: Huelvia–Garston. CARGO: ore.
SINKING: 24th May 1913.
LOCATION: lat 51° 43′ 07″ N. long 05° 40′ 10″ W. (E).
DEPTH: bottom 60′–70′.   SURVEYS: RN.

Wreck 305. Unknown
LOCATION: lat 51° 43′ 55″ N. long 05° 28′ 47″ W. (E).
ADDITIONAL: First located by divers in 1967, who reported 'A large unknown vessel sunk just north of the north-west tip of Grassholm Island.' No other details.

Wreck 306. Unknown
LOCATION: lat 51° 43′ 44″ N. long 05° 28′ 32″ W. (E).
SURVEYS: subaqua.
ADDITIONAL: First located by divers in 1968. The wreck of a largish ship, about 2000 t., the wreckage is about 120′ in length. It looks as though some salvage has taken place in the past.

Wreck 307. Steamship WHITEPLAIN
LOCATION: lat 51° 51′ 01″ N. long 05° 17′ 08″ W.
No other details, except that this vessel and position was first reported in April 1969.

Wreck 308. Steamship LONSDALE
TONNAGE: 500 t.g.
LOCATION: lat 51° 44′ 09″ N. long 05° 15′ 44″ W.
ADDITIONAL: This wreck was first located in October 1968, by divers. The wreckage stands some 9′ high, and some salvage has taken place in the past. A coaster, the name of the wreck is that given by locals, and is unconfirmed.

Wreck 309. Steamer MOLESEY
DIMENSIONS: 347·8 × 49·5 × 25·5.   TONNAGE: 3809 t.g.
BUILT: 1899.   SINKING: 24th November 1929.
LOCATION: lat 51° 44′ 02″ N. long 05° 15′ 39″ W. (E).
DEPTH: height 25′.   SURVEYS: subaqua.
ADDITIONAL: This vessel ran into a 70 mph gale, which broke the propeller. After dropping anchor it ran aground (both anchors dragged) then slid back into the sea. Latest subaqua reports state that some 'inexpert' salvage has taken place; the whole wreck is covered with heavy weed growth.

Wreck 310. British schooner PERSEVERANCE
SINKING: 21st May 1932.
LOCATION: lat 51° 44′ 00″ N. long 05° 18′ 45″ W.
ADDITIONAL: Foundered in Pinkstone Bay (Skomer Island). No other details.

Wreck 311. Schooner ENGLISHMAN
TONNAGE: 144 t.g. 118 t.n.   BUILT: 1864 at Lancaster.
OWNERS: G. H. Dudderidge Jr (who was captain at time of loss).
CARGO: china clay.   SINKING: 2nd May 1933.
LOCATION: lat 51° 44′ 32″ N. long 05° 12′ 53″ W. (E).

DEPTH: least 38′. SURVEYS: RN.
ADDITIONAL: Struck an obstruction before sinking.

Wreck 312. Unknown
LOCATION: lat 51° 44′ 05·5″ N. long 05° 15′ 38″ W. (E).
DEPTH: bottom 60′. SURVEYS: RN.
ADDITIONAL: First located in 1967, this is a large wreck.

Wreck 313. Cable ship FARADAY
DIMENSIONS: 394·3 × 48·3 × 34·6. TONNAGE: 5533 t.g.
ROUTE: Falmouth–Milford Haven.
CARGO: 3870 t. submarine cable. SINKING 26/27th March 1941.
LOCATION: lat 51° 42′ 40″ N. long 05° 12′ 12″ W. (E).
SURVEYS: RN; subaqua.
ADDITIONAL: The bottom is of large boulders, and the wreck is lying in them. The sea action has resulted in the wreck breaking up, but many tons of cable in pyramid piles 6′ high are around. Heavy tides limit this one to the experienced diver.

Wreck 314. British liner DAKOTIAN
TONNAGE: 6426 t.g. CARGO: general, and tin plate.
SINKING: 21st November 1940.
LOCATION: lat 51° 42′ 12″ N. long 05° 08′ 18″ W. (E).
DEPTH: bottom 50′. HEIGHT: 30′. SURVEYS: RN; subaqua.
ADDITIONAL: This wreck is lying on an even keel and seems structurally sound.

Wreck 315. Greek steamship NICOLAOU VIRGINIA
TONNAGE: 6869 t.g. BUILT: 1920.
CARGO: grain. SINKING: 27th March 1946.
LOCATION: lat 51° 36′ 18″ N. long 05° 01′ 30″ W. (E).
DEPTH: bottom 30′–40′. HEIGHT: 15′. SURVEYS: RN; subaqua.
ADDITIONAL: First located in 1968. The wreck is in very good condition, hull only slightly broken up and engine, machinery, boilers etc, are all intact. The reason why it is not very 'tall' is because it is sunk well into the sea bed.

Wreck 316. KELVINIA
TONNAGE: 5039 t.g. SINKING: 2nd September 1916.
LOCATION: lat 51° 33′ 38″ N. long 04° 42′ 30″ W. (E).
DEPTH: bottom 105′, least 60′. SURVEYS: RN 1964.
No other details.

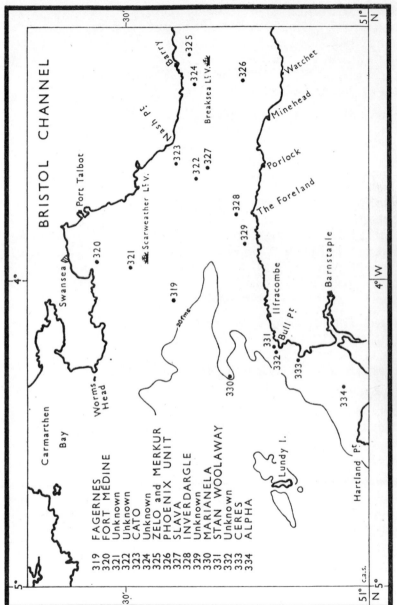

BRISTOL CHANNEL

Carmarthen
Bay

Worms
Head

Swansea

Port Talbot

Nash Pt.

Barry

Scarweather Lt.V.

Breaksea Lt.V.

•320
•321

•323
•322

•324 •325
•327
•326

Minehead

Watchet

Porlock

The Foreland

•328
•329

Ilfracombe

Bull Pt.

Barnstaple

20 Fms.

•319

330•

331•
332•
333•

334•

Lundy I.

Hartland Pt.

319 FAGERNES
320 FORT MEDINE
321 Unknown
322 Unknown
323 CATO
324 Unknown
325 ZELO and MERKUR
326 PHOENIX UNIT
327 SLAVA
328 INVERDARGLE
329 Unknown
330 MARIANELA
331 STAN WOOLAWAY
332 Unknown
333 CERES
334 ALPHA

5°
4°
4° W

51° c.a.s.
N 5°

N

30'—
—30'

51°
N

Chart 19   Bristol Channel

Wreck 317. British cargo steamship JUNTA
DIMENSIONS: 245 × 36·7 × 16.   TONNAGE: 1559 t.g.
BUILT: 1908.   ROUTE: Rouen–Glasgow.
SINKING: 7th October 1945.
LOCATION: lat 51° 37' 48" N. long 04° 39' 18" W. (E).
DEPTH: bottom 60'.   SURVEYS: RN.

Wreck 318. British motor vessel LADY SHEILA
TONNAGE: 200 t.g.   SINKING: 29th November 1954.
LOCATION: lat 51° 34' 50" N. long 04° 31' 23" W. (E). Or,
B & D from Caldy Island Light, 117° 6·7 miles.
DEPTH: bottom 90', least 78'.   SURVEYS: RN.

Wreck 319. Italian steamship FAGERNES
DIMENSIONS: 305 × 43·7 × 27·2.   TONNAGE: 3204 t.g.
BUILT: 1916.   CARGO: 4500 t. coal.
SINKING: 17 March 1923.
LOCATION: lat 51° 23' 54" N. long 04° 03' 36" W. (E).
DEPTH: bottom 111', least 90'.   SURVEYS: RN.
ADDITIONAL: Sunk in collision.

Wreck 320. French oil fuelled vessel FORT MÉDINE
TONNAGE: 5355 t.g.   SINKING: 3rd March 1941.
LOCATION: lat 51° 33' 22" N. long 03° 56' 18" W. (E).
DEPTH: bottom 55'–60', least 45'.   SURVEYS: HMS Seagull.

Wreck 321. Unknown
LOCATION: lat 51° 29' 30" N. long 03° 57' 45" W. (E).
DEPTH: bottom 65'–75'.   SURVEYS: RN 1940, 1955.
ADDITIONAL: This is presumed to be an early World War Two
wreck.

Wreck 322. Unknown
LOCATION: lat 51° 21' 09" N. long 03° 40' 24" W. (E).
DEPTH: bottom 66'–70', least 45'.   SURVEYS: HMS Seagull 1949.
ADDITIONAL: First located during the 1949 survey.

Wreck 323. British steamship CATO
DIMENSIONS: 231 × 30·9 × 19.   TONNAGE: 710 t.g.
BUILT: 1914.   ROUTE: Dublin–Bristol.
SINKING: 3rd March 1940.
LOCATION: lat 51° 23' 38" N. long 03° 37' 32" W. (E).
DEPTH: bottom 55–65', least 38'.   SURVEYS: HMS Cook.

Wreck 324. Unknown
LOCATION: lat 51° 21′ 24″ N. long 03° 21′ 26″ W. (E).
DEPTH: bottom 65′–75′, least 36′. SURVEYS: HMS Scott.
ADDITIONAL: This wreck was first located in 1941. It is presumed to be a World War Two loss.

Wreck 325. ZELO
SINKING: 19th September 1920.
LOCATION: lat 51° 21′ 56″ N. long 03° 16′ 00″ W. (E).
DEPTH: bottom 45′–55′, least 39′. SURVEYS: HMS Woodlark 1969.
ADDITIONAL: This wreckage is combined with that of Wreck 325a.

Wreck 325a. MERKUR
No details available apart from name. This wreckage is combined with that of Wreck 325.

Wreck 326. Phoenix Unit
LOCATION: lat 51° 15′ 44″ N. long 03° 21′ 09″ W. (E).
DEPTH: bottom 45′–50′, least 36′.
ADDITIONAL: Sunk at the end of World War Two. Although not a true 'wreck', Phoenix Units, by their very construction, usually contain prolific marine life.

Wreck 327. Yugoslav steamship SLAVA
DIMENSIONS: 369·5 × 50 × 26·3. TONNAGE: 4512 t.g.
BUILT: 1911. SINKING: 17th March 1940.
LOCATION: lat 51° 19′ 52″ N. long 03° 38′ 11″ W. (E).
DEPTH: bottom 70′–72′, least 48′. SURVEYS: Trinity House.

Wreck 328. British tanker INVERDARGLE
DIMENSIONS: 503·2 × 67·3 × 34·2. TONNAGE: 9456 t.g.
BUILT: 1938. ROUTE: Trinidad–Avonmouth.
CARGO: aviation spirit. SINKING: 19th January 1940.
LOCATION: lat 51° 16′ 31″ N. long 03° 47′ 20″ W. (E).
DEPTH: bottom 72′–75′, least 47′. SURVEYS: HMS Seagull.
ADDITIONAL: The cause of sinking (explosion) is not known, but is presumed to have been a mine or torpedo.

Wreck 329. Unknown
LOCATION: lat 51° 15′ 27″ N. long 03° 52′ 58″ W. (E).
DEPTH: bottom 60′–65′, least 49′. SURVEYS: RN 1950.
ADDITIONAL: Presumed to be a World War Two wreck.

335	RADYR	355	GEMINI	
336	MOLIERE	356	Unknown	
337	POITIERS	357	Unknown	
338	CLANGULA	358	ENRICO PARODI	
339	RIMFAKSE	359	LIBERTY	
340	Unknown	360	BEAUMARIS	
341	ST. GEORGES			
342	GIRDLENESS			
343	Unknown			
344	MILLY			
345	ARTHURTOWN			
346	Unknown			
347	SAPHIR			
348	POLDOWN			
349	TAGONA			
350	ONEGA			
351	LAVERNOCK			
352	LAKE EDEN			
353	CRISTINA			
354	REINO			

HARTLAND P^t TO LANDS END

Chart 20   Hartland Point to Land's End

Wreck 330. Steamship MARIANELA
TONNAGE: 748 t.g.   SINKING: 1921.
LOCATION: lat 51° 17′ 20″ N. long 04° 19′ 05″ W.
DEPTH: bottom 117′.   SURVEYS: RN 1921.
ADDITIONAL: A survey ship located a wreck at this position in 1921; it was presumed to be the Marianela, but this has never been confirmed.

Wreck 331. Sand dredger STAN WOOLAWAY
DIMENSIONS: 142 × 26 × 8.   TONNAGE: 278 t.g.
CARGO: sand.   SINKING: 13th March 1967.
LOCATION: lat 51° 11′ 57″ N. long 04° 13′ 00″ W. (E).
DEPTH: least 36′.   SURVEYS: Trinity House 1969.

Wreck 332. Unknown
LOCATION: lat 51° 11′ 39″ N. long 04° 14′ 18″ W. (E).
DEPTH: least 24′.
ADDITIONAL: This wreck was first located by the steamship Barford in 1918, and confirmed in the same year by the steamship Ausable (USA). However, several subaqua clubs have tried to locate it without success.

Wreck 333. CERES
SINKING: pre-1937.
LOCATION: lat 51° 08′ 54″ N. long 04° 15′ 36″ W. (A).
ADDITIONAL: The records of Customs and Receiver of Wrecks report the sinking as near Baggy Point, without being specific about the date. In 1948 Trinity House surveyed the area but could not locate the wreck owing to adverse conditions.

Wreck 334. ALPHA
SINKING: 1930.
LOCATION: lat 51° 03′ 08″ N. long 04° 21′ 00″ W. (E).
DEPTH: bottom 60′, least 43′.   SURVEYS: RN.
ADDITIONAL: In 1957 the masts and rigging were removed as a danger to shipping.

Wreck 335. British steamship RADYR
DIMENSIONS: 235 × 42 × 19.   TONNAGE: 2357 t.g.
BUILT: 1918 by Harland & Wolf.   ROUTE: Cardiff–Bordeaux.
CARGO: 2799 t. coal.   SINKING: 7th December 1924.
LOCATION: lat 51° 01′ 00″ N. long 04° 32′ 00″ W. (A).
DEPTH: bottom 45′–50′.

91

ADDITIONAL: Ran into a NW gale with engine trouble. Last seen in Bigbury Bay in position given. Some wreckage was washed ashore.

Wreck 336. French steamship MOLIÈRE
DIMENSIONS: 265·2 × 35·5 × 6·8.   TONNAGE: 1545 t.g.
BUILT: 1882.   SINKING: 25th May 1918.
LOCATION: lat 51° 01′ 06″ N. long 04° 34′ 24″ W. (E).
DEPTH: bottom 90′.   SURVEYS: HMS Beaufort 1921.
ADDITIONAL: From records available, it is presumed that this is the Molière. The wreck was located in 1921 and the position was confirmed in 1966.

Wreck 337. French steamship POITIERS
DIMENSIONS: 251 × 43·8 × 18·2.   TONNAGE: 2042 t.g.
BUILT: 1917.   SINKING: 28th April 1918.
LOCATION: lat 50° 59′ 00″ N. long 04° 36′ 00″ W. (A).
DEPTH: bottom 100′ approx.

Wreck 338. British steamship CLANGULA
DIMENSIONS: 285 × 40 × 19·4.   TONNAGE: 1754 t.g.
BUILT: 1917.   SINKING: 17th November 1917.
LOCATION: lat 50° 58′ 00″ N. long 04° 35′ 00″ W. (A).
DEPTH: bottom 90′–110′ approx.
ADDITIONAL: Torpedoed only one month after launching.

Wreck 339. Norwegian merchant steamship RIMFAKSE
DIMENSIONS: 229 × 35·2 × 15·9.   TONNAGE: 649 t.g.
BUILT: 1909.   CARGO: 1600 t. iron ore.
SINKING: 28th April 1918.
LOCATION: lat 50° 55′ 03″ N. long 04° 36′ 00″ W. (A).
DEPTH: bottom 80′–85′ approx.

Wreck 340. Unknown
LOCATION: lat 50° 51′ 00″ N. long 04° 37′ 00″ W. (A).
ADDITIONAL: This information came from a report by the British steamship Muldistone that it had seen a steamer, believed French, sink in this position on 2nd May 1918. It sank in four minutes.

Wreck 341. French steamship ST GEORGES
DIMENSIONS: 180·1 × 27·1 × 14 depth (not draught).
TONNAGE: 633 t.g.   ROUTE: Penarth–Rouen.
CARGO: coal.   SINKING: 17th July 1918.
LOCATION: lat 50° 46′ 50″ N. long 04° 37′ 50″ W. (A).

DEPTH: bottom 83′ approx.
ADDITIONAL: Torpedoed by a German submarine, this wreck has never been located.

Wreck 342. British merchant steamship GIRDLENESS
DIMENSIONS: 330·1 × 46 × 24·4 depth. TONNAGE: 3018 t.g.
BUILT: 1905. ROUTE: Swansea–?. CARGO: fuel.
SINKING: 2nd May 1918.
LOCATION: lat 50° 46′ 00″ N. long 04° 40′ 45″ W. (A).
ADDITIONAL: Thirty days after the Girdleness sank, the steamship Milly (see Wreck 344) reported 'I have fouled the wreck of the Girdleness', in the above position. However, a search by Trinity House to confirm the position was unsuccessful.

Wreck 343. Unknown
LOCATION: lat 50° 45′ 00″ N. long 04° 44′ 56″ W. (E).
DEPTH: bottom 120′.
ADDITIONAL: All that is known is a report in 1905 which stated 'Mast is still visible, but vessel is sinking.'

Wreck 344. MILLY
TONNAGE: 2963 t.g. SINKING: 6th September 1918.
LOCATION: lat 50° 39′ 00″ N. long 04° 51′ 00″ W. (A).
ADDITIONAL: Milly was torpedoed and sank in 5 minutes. A 1918 report said that it had been located in 60′ of water, but this remains unconfirmed.

Wreck 345. Steamship ARTHURTOWN
SINKING: World War Two.
LOCATION: lat 50° 34′ 15″ N. long 04° 57′ 36″ W. (E).
DEPTH: bottom 75′. HEIGHT: 20′. SURVEYS: RN; subaqua.
ADDITIONAL: First located by the RN in 1959, who reported 'Mast is just visible at low water.' Divers in 1969 reported 'Wreck stands upright with the holds still intact, but blocked solid with cargo of scrap iron. Engines intact and upright in stern; bows NE.'

Wreck 346. Unknown
LOCATION: lat 50° 35′ 54″ N. long 04° 59′ 52″ W. (E).
DEPTH: bottom 105′, least 51′. SURVEYS: HMS Beaufort 1932.
ADDITIONAL: First located during the 1932 survey. Obviously a large wreck.

Wreck 347. Norwegian steamship SAPHIR
DIMENSIONS: 245·3 × 36·3 × 16·9. TONNAGE: 1406 t.g. 841 t.n.
BUILT: 1901 of steel. CARGO: coal. SINKING: 25th May 1918.
LOCATION: lat 50° 34' 27" N. long 05° 04' 26" W. (E).
DEPTH: bottom 104', least 48'. SURVEYS: RN.

Wreck 348. Armed British merchant steamship POLDOWN
DIMENSIONS: 229·7 × 35 × 21·8. TONNAGE: 1379 t.g. 849 t.n.
BUILT: 1904 of steel. CARGO: 1515 t. coal.
SINKING: 9th October 1917.
LOCATION: lat 50° 31' 35" N. long 05° 05' 05" W. (E).
DEPTH: bottom 90'–100', least 60'. SURVEYS: RN.

Wreck 349. Armed British merchant steamship TAGONA
DIMENSIONS: 249·6 × 42·6 × 21·1. TONNAGE: 2004 t.g. 1229 t.n.
BUILT: 1908, of steel, by A. A. Milne & Sons. CARGO: iron ore.
OWNERS: Canadian Steamship Lines. SINKING: 16th May 1918.
LOCATION: lat 50° 30' 08" N. long 05° 07' 01" W. (E).
ADDITIONAL: This wreck was located by a lone diver in 1967,
and as far as is known it has been purchased by him.

Wreck 350. Armed British merchant steamship ONEGA
DIMENSIONS: 401 × 39·6 × 21·3. TONNAGE: 3636 t.g. 2276 t.n.
BUILT: 1880, of steel, by Harland & Wolf.
SINKING: 30th August 1918.
LOCATION: lat 50° 28' 50" N. long 05° 00' 08" W. (A).
DEPTH: bottom 97' approx.

Wreck 351. British merchant steamship LAVERNOCK
DIMENSIONS: 275 × 40·3 × 20·9. TONNAGE: 2406 t.g. 1496 t.n.
BUILT: 1888, of steel, by Palmers. CARGO: iron ore.
SINKING: 17th September 1918.
LOCATION: lat 50° 28' 30" N. long 05° 05' 42" W. (A).

Wreck 352. US merchant steamship LAKE EDEN
DIMENSIONS: 251 × 43·5 × 24·2. TONNAGE: 2371 t.g. 1451 t.n.
BUILT: 1918 by American SBC. SINKING: 24th August 1918.
LOCATION: lat 50° 28' 15" N. long 05° 08' 00" W. (E).
DEPTH: bottom 114', least 90'. SURVEYS: RN.

Wreck 353. Spanish merchant steamship CRISTINA
DIMENSIONS: 281·7 × 40 × 19·2. TONNAGE: 2083 t.g.
BUILT: 1903. SINKING: 10th March 1918.

LOCATION: lat 50° 23' 00" N. long 05° 11' 00" W. (A).
DEPTH: bottom 70'–90' approx.

Wreck 354. Merchant steamship REINO (or REIME)
TONNAGE: 1913 t.g.   SINKING: 7th November 1916.
LOCATION: lat 50° 17' 06" N. long 05° 27' 00" W. (E).
DEPTH: bottom 75'–80', least 60'.
SURVEYS: HMS Beaufort 1930.
ADDITIONAL: This wreck was first located by HMS Beaufort in 1930.

Wreck 355. British merchant steamship GEMINI
TONNAGE: 2128 t.g.   SINKING: 20th July 1918.
LOCATION: lat 50° 17' 30" N. long 05° 38' 30" W. (E).
DEPTH: bottom 104', least 60'.   SURVEYS: RN.

Wreck 356. Unknown
LOCATION: lat 50° 16' 00" N. long 05° 29' 02" W. (E).
DEPTH: bottom 75'–85', least 54'.   SURVEYS: HMS Beaufort.
ADDITIONAL: This wreck was first located in 1918, and is presumed to have sunk that year. An unconfirmed report suggests that it might be the steamship ST CHAMOND.

Wreck 357. Unknown
LOCATION: lat 50° 14' 23" N. long 05° 28' 40" W. (E).
DEPTH: bottom 70'–75', least 54'.
SURVEYS: HMS Lark; HMS Beaufort.
ADDITIONAL: First located by a trawler in 1918, and confirmed by the two surveys. Presumed sunk in 1918.

Wreck 358. Steamship ENRICO PARODI
TONNAGE: 3818 t.g.   SINKING: 1916.
LOCATION: lat 50° 13' 00" N. long 05° 33' 15" W. (E).
DEPTH: bottom 60'–65', least 39'.   SURVEYS: RN.

Wreck 359. Steamship LIBERTY
TONNAGE: 5250 t.g.   SINKING: 17th January 1952.
LOCATION: lat 50° 10' 00" N. long 05° 39' 52" W.
DEPTH: bottom 50' approx.

Wreck 360. Steamship BEAUMARIS
TONNAGE: 2372 t.g.   SINKING: 7th February 1918.
LOCATION: lat 50° 04' 50" N. long 05° 42' 00" W.
DEPTH: bottom 50'.   SURVEYS: RN; subaqua.
ADDITIONAL: Some salvage operations were carried out in 1925

THE SCILLY ISLES

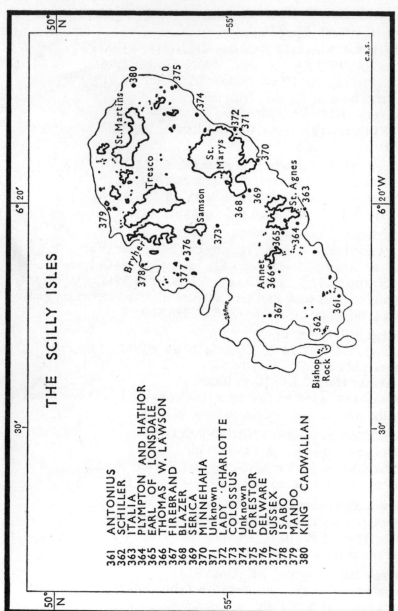

361 ANTONIUS
362 SCHILLER
363 ITALIA
364 PLYMPTON AND HATHOR
365 EARL OF LONSDALE
366 THOMAS W. LAWSON
367 FIREBRAND
368 BLAZER
369 SERICA
370 MINNEHAHA
371 Unknown
372 LADY CHARLOTTE
373 COLOSSUS
374 Unknown
375 FORESTOR
376 DELWARE
377 SUSSEX
378 ISABO
379 MANDO
380 KING CADWALLAN

Chart 21   The Scilly Isles

to remove the mast and funnels. The derrick is still visible at low water. This wreck has been purchased.

Wreck 361. Greek steamship ANTONIUS
DIMENSIONS: 328 × 41 × 16.   TONNAGE: 2626 t.g.
BUILT: 1894.   CARGO: sugar.   SINKING: 8th December 1912.
LOCATION: lat 49° 51′ 45″ N. long 06° 21′ 09″ W. (E).
DEPTH: bottom 70′–100′.   SURVEYS: RN.
ADDITIONAL: Registered in Andros. Wrecked on a rock called Old Bess, and now well broken up around the rock.

Wreck 362. German iron steamship SCHILLER
DIMENSIONS: 380 × 40 × 24.   TONNAGE: 2326 t.g.
BUILT: 1873.   CARGO: bullion.
OWNERS: Transatlantic SN Co.   SINKING: 8th May 1875.
LOCATION: lat 49° 52′ 10″ N. long 06° 25′ 40″ W. (E).
ADDITIONAL: Wrecked on Retarrier Ledge. This is a dangerous area, and although the wreck is still recognisable there is very little left owing to salvage.

Wreck 363. Steamship steel screw schooner ITALIA
TONNAGE: 2792 t.g.   ROUTE: Cardiff–Taranto.
CARGO: coal.   SINKING: May 1917.
LOCATION: lat 49° 52′ 48″ N. long 06° 20′ 14″ W. (E).
DEPTH: bottom (bow) 30′, (stern) 120′.   SURVEYS: subaqua.
ADDITIONAL: This wreck is dived regularly. The hull is virtually intact with little evidence of silting. A 40 mm gun was recovered in 1965.

Wreck 364. German steamship HATHOR
DIMENSIONS: 472 × 61 × 28·5.   TONNAGE: 7060 t.g.
ROUTE: Africa–Portland.   CARGO: oil cake and nitrate of potash.
SINKING: 2nd December 1920.
LOCATION: lat 49° 53′ 00″ N. long 06° 20′ 50″ W. (E).
ADDITIONAL: This wreckage is combined with that of Wreck 364a (Plympton). The Hathor is lying across the wreck of the Plympton, much broken up. The bows of the Plympton are upside down.

Wreck 364a. British steamship PLYMPTON
DIMENSIONS: 314 × 40·5 × 21.   TONNAGE: 2869 t.g.
BUILT: 1893 by Furness Withy.   SINKING: 14th August 1909.
ADDITIONAL: This wreckage is combined with that of Wreck 364.

Wreck 365. Steamship EARL OF LONSDALE
CARGO: cotton seed. SINKING: 8th June 1885.
LOCATION: lat 49° 53′ 25″ N. long 06° 21′ 17″ W. (E).
SURVEYS: subaqua.
ADDITIONAL: The wreckage is spread some 200 ft northward from Carnew Rock.

Wreck 366. American schooner THOMAS W. LAWSON
TONNAGE: 5006 t.g. BUILT: 1902.
ROUTE: Philadelphia–London. CARGO: 6000 t. petroleum.
SINKING: 13th December 1907.
LOCATION: lat 49° 53′ 39″ N. long 06° 23′ 08″ W. (E).
SURVEYS: subaqua.
ADDITIONAL: The Thomas W. Lawson, a seven-masted schooner, was the largest sailing vessel built. And as far as is known only two seven-masted schooners were ever made.

Wreck 367. FIREBRAND
SINKING: 22nd October 1707.
LOCATION: lat 49° 53′ 45″ N. long 06° 25′ 02″ W. (E).
DEPTH: bottom 50′–70′. SURVEYS: subaqua.
ADDITIONAL: This vessel sank along with the 'Association Fleet', on hitting Gunners Ledge. It was a fireship. The area of the wreck is approx. 200′ × 100′.

Wreck 368. Tug BLAZER
SINKING: 11th November 1918.
LOCATION: lat 49° 54′ 34″ N. long 06° 19′ 40″ W. (E).
DEPTH: bottom 27′, least 7′. SURVEYS: HMS Drake.
ADDITIONAL: The bottom consists of bed rock and weed. Someone is currently negotiating to buy this wreck.

Wreck 369. Steamship SERICA
TONNAGE: 1736 t.g. BUILT: 1888.
ROUTE: Cardiff–Port Said. CARGO: coal.
SINKING: 24th November 1893.
LOCATION: lat 49° 54′ 24″ N. long 06° 19′ 25″ W. (E).
DEPTH: bottom 40′. SURVEYS: subaqua.

Wreck 370. Barquentine MINNEHAHA
DIMENSIONS: 158 × 33·7 × 22·4. TONNAGE: 845 t.g.
ROUTE: Falmouth–Dublin. CARGO: guano.
SINKING: 7th July 1871.

LOCATION: lat 49° 54′ 10″ N. long 06° 18′ 04″ W. (E).
DEPTH: bottom 30′–60′. SURVEYS: subaqua.
ADDITIONAL: This wreck was located by divers, who found two large anchors, capstan, chain, iron beams, etc. This four-masted barquentine is sometimes confused with another Minnehaha which sank in 1910 and was later refloated.

Wreck 371. Unknown
LOCATION: lat 49° 54′ 40″ N. long 06° 16′ 40″ W. (E).
DEPTH: bottom 120′. SURVEYS: subaqua 1966.
ADDITIONAL: Located by divers, who reported 'Found two huge anchors, once wooden stocked, both shanks 14′ long and the rings 3′ outside diameter. Must have been a large vessel.'

Wreck 372. Steamship LADY CHARLOTTE
DIMENSIONS: 348·7 × 50·1 × 20·1. TONNAGE: 3953 t.g. 3368 t.n.
BUILT: 1905. CARGO: coal. SINKING: 14th May 1917.
LOCATION: lat 49° 54′ 50″ N. long 06° 16′ 40″ W. (E). Or, B & D from the end of Porthellick Point, 140° 250 ft.
DEPTH: bottom 30′–85′. SURVEYS: subaqua.
ADDITIONAL: Divers report that the wreck is breaking up, but the stern (in 85′) and boiler are intact.

Wreck 373. HMS COLOSSUS
SINKING: 10th December 1798.
LOCATION: lat 49° 55′ 19″ N. long 06° 21′ 02″ W. (E).
DEPTH: bottom 10′–50′. SURVEYS: RN; subaqua.
ADDITIONAL: This 74-gun vessel parted a cable, dragged two anchors, and grounded on a rock. Local divers have recovered some guns, which have been placed in the garrison. There was a cargo of ancient vases from the collection of Sir William Hamilton which is still unlocated. The wreck area is approx. 200′ in radius.

Wreck 374. Unknown
LOCATION: lat 49° 56′ 00″ N. long 06° 16′ 00″ W. (E).
DEPTH: bottom 90′, least 72′. SURVEYS: HMS Spencer.
ADDITIONAL: This wreck was first located by a RN survey ship in 1888; the position was confirmed this century by HMS Spencer. As it is still a substantial size for this length of time, it should be well worth a visit.

Wreck 375. HM brigantine HMS FORESTOR
ROUTE: Plymouth–Africa. SINKING: 13th February 1833.
LOCATION: lat 49° 56′ 37″ N. long 06° 14′ 42″ W. (E).
DEPTH: bottom 30′–40′. SURVEYS: subaqua 1966.
ADDITIONAL: This wreck was first located by divers in 1966.
There is a considerable quantity of cannon in the area.

Wreck 376. Steamship DELAWARE
ROUTE: Liverpool-Calcutta. CARGO: silk.
SINKING: 20th December 1871.
LOCATION: lat 49° 56′ 14″ N. long 06° 22′ 30″ W. (E).
DEPTH: bottom 30′–50′. SURVEYS: RN.
ADDITIONAL: Wrecked at a site now named the Delaware
Ledges.

Wreck 377. Steamship SUSSEX
ROUTE: Baltimore–London. CARGO: 2000 head of cattle.
SINKING: 17th December 1885.
LOCATION: lat 49° 56′ 32″ N. long 06° 23′ 13″ W. (E).
DEPTH: bottom 20′–30′. SURVEYS: RN; subaqua.
ADDITIONAL: The remains are scattered around the base of Seal
Rock.

Wreck 378. Steamer ISABO
DIMENSIONS: 422 × 54 × 27·4. TONNAGE: 6827 t.g.
BUILT: 1914. ROUTE: Montreal–Trieste.
CARGO: grain. SINKING: 27th October 1927.
LOCATION: lat 49° 57′ 30″ N. long 06° 22′ 47″ W.
DEPTH: bottom 30′–50′. SURVEYS: subaqua.
ADDITIONAL: Local divers report that the bows are S. They
also gave a position that varies slightly from the above (31″ N.
53″ W) in which they found either part of the Isabo or a smaller
wreck.

Wreck 379. Panamanian steamship MANDO
DIMENSIONS: 422 × 57 × 34. TONNAGE: 7176 t.g.
BUILT: 1944. ROUTE: Hampton Roads–Rotterdam.
CARGO: coal. SINKING: 21st January 1955.
LOCATION: lat 49° 58′ 27″ N. long 06° 20′ 15″ W. (E).
DEPTH: bottom (bow) 40′, (stern) 100′. SURVEYS: subaqua.
ADDITIONAL: This is reported to be an excellent dive. 'The wreck
lies SE–NW and is 400 feet long.' Fairly well broken up, divers
have recovered the 9 t. phosphor bronze propeller.

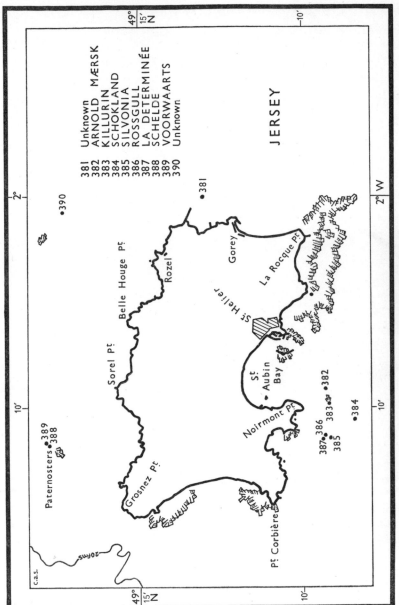

381 Unknown
382 ARNOLD MÆRSK
383 KILLURIN
384 SCHOKLAND
385 SILVONIA
386 ROSSGULL
387 LA DETERMINÉE
388 SCHELDE
389 VOORWAARTS
390 Unknown

JERSEY

Paternosters 389
388

Grosnez Pt.

Pt. Corbière

Noirmont Pt.

St. Aubin Bay

387 386
385
383 382
384

Sorel Pt.

Belle Houge Pt.

Rozel

Gorey

St. Helier

La Rocque Pt.

381

390

C.a.s.

20 fms.

Chart 22   Jersey

101

Wreck 380. Steamer KING CADWALLAN (or CADWAILEN)
DIMENSIONS: 326 × 28 × 23. TONNAGE: 3275 t.g. BUILT: 1900.
ROUTE: Cardiff–Naples. CARGO: coal. OWNERS: King Line.
SINKING: 29th July 1906 (some unconfirmed reports say 1904).
LOCATION: lat 49° 57' 58" N. long 06° 14' 34" W.
DEPTH: bottom 80'–100'. SURVEYS: subaqua.
ADDITIONAL: Reported to be a good dive. Some salvage, but otherwise intact. A single-screw steamer.

Wreck 381. Unknown
LOCATION: lat 49° 13' 00" N. long 02° 00' 00" W.
DEPTH: bottom 30'–40'. SURVEYS: RN.
ADDITIONAL: First located in 1927.

Wreck 382. German steamship ARNOLD MÆRSK
DIMENSIONS: 280 × 40. TONNAGE: 1966 t.g.
SINKING: 22nd May 1943.
LOCATION: lat 49° 19' 14" N. long 02° 19' 08" W. (E).
DEPTH: bottom 30'. SURVEYS: subaqua.
ADDITIONAL: This wreck is broken up and the remains are combined with another, unknown, wreck. The Mærsk was a Danish ship under the control of Germany after the occupation of Denmark.

Wreck 383. Tug KILLURIN
TONNAGE: 565 t.g. SINKING: February 1950.
LOCATION: lat 49° 19' 10" N. long 02° 09' 50" W.
DEPTH: bottom 30'. SURVEYS: subaqua.
ADDITIONAL: Reported to be a good dive. The vessel is broken up, and the propeller is missing. However, a differing position has been given from that mentioned (14" N. 42" W).

Wreck 384. Dutch steamship SCHOKLAND
TONNAGE: 1113 t.g.
LOCATION: lat 49° 08' 22" N. long 02° 10' 30" W. (E).
DEPTH: bottom 72', least 34'. SURVEYS: HMS Medina; subaqua.
ADDITIONAL: The wreck is lying in an E–W direction and is about 275' long. The bows are upright with little damage to hull apart from a dent in the stern and a 15'–20' gash in the starboard forward section, but this cannot be seen easily. The Germans in World War Two removed materials and guns from the stern hold.

Wreck 385. British steamship SILVONIA
DIMENSIONS: 211·3 × 33·2 × 13·1. TONNAGE: 1131 t.g.
BUILT: 1930. CARGO: coal. SINKING: 6th May 1935.
LOCATION: lat 49° 09′ 06″ N. long 02° 11′ 28″ W. Or, B & D
from Hubaut Rock, 122° 2 cables.
ADDITIONAL: Fairly well broken up. Engine block is broken in
half and all non-ferrous metals have disappeared. The propeller
(iron) is still intact.

Wreck 386. Steamship ROSSGULL
SINKING: 4th December 1900.
LOCATION: lat 49° 19′ 10″ N. long 02° 11′ 20″ W.
SURVEYS: subaqua.
ADDITIONAL: This wreck lies approx. 200 yd ENE of Wreck 385.
The bows are NW, most of the plating has rusted away but the
winch, crane, engine and a small section of the stern are all
complete, as is the (iron) propeller.

Wreck 387. Frigate HMS LA DETERMINÉE
TONNAGE: 544 t.g. SINKING: 26th March 1803.
LOCATION: lat 40° 19′ 16″ N. long 02° 11′ 26″ W.
DEPTH: bottom 30′–50′. SURVEYS: subaqua.
ADDITIONAL: This 22-gun vessel was wrecked after striking a
sunken rock. The wreck was located by a diver, a Mr Tittering-
ton, who purchased it.

Wreck 388. SCHELDE
SINKING: before 1939.
LOCATION: lat 49° 17′ 48″ N. long 02° 11′ 40″ W.
ADDITIONAL: This wreck lies very close to Wreck 389.

Wreck 389. VOORWAARTS
TONNAGE: 261 t.g. SINKING: 23rd March 1950.
LOCATION: lat 49° 17′ 53″ N. long 02° 11′ 40″ W.
DEPTH: bottom 30′. SURVEYS: subaqua.
ADDITIONAL: Fairly well broken up, this wreck has been
purchased by a Mr D. Parks.

Wreck 390. Unknown
LOCATION: lat 40° 17′ 20″ N. long 02° 00′ 41″ W.
DEPTH: bottom 48′–50′. SURVEYS: RN.
ADDITIONAL: Only that this wreck was first located in 1928.

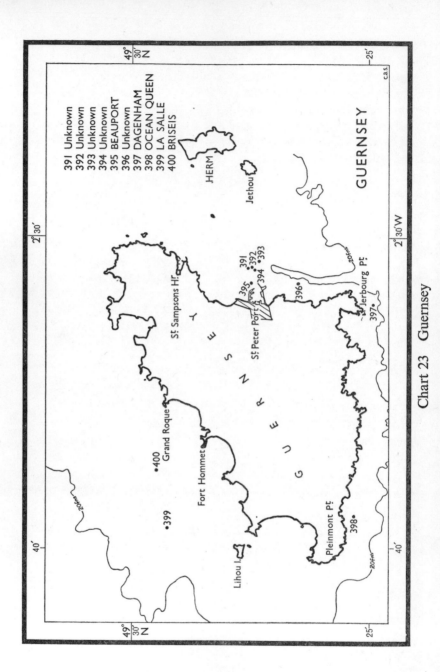

391 Unknown
392 Unknown
393 Unknown
394 Unknown
395 BEAUPORT
396 Unknown
397 DAGENHAM
398 OCEAN QUEEN
399 LA SALLE
400 BRISEIS

HERM

Jethou

GUERNSEY

St Sampsons Hr

St Peter Port

Grand Roque

Fort Hommet

Lihou I.

Pleinmont Pt

•400

•399

398•

391
392 •393
395 •394

396•

Jerbourg Pt
397•

G U E R N S E Y

Chart 23   Guernsey

104

Wreck 391. Unknown

LOCATION: lat 49° 27' 33" N. long 02° 30' 58" W.

DEPTH: least 45'. SURVEYS: subaqua.

ADDITIONAL: Thought to be a trawler-type vessel by the divers who located it. Sitting upright, the remains are nearly 130' in length. A warning note—there was ammunition on this wreck and some of it was removed (a dangerous procedure).

Wreck 392. Unknown

LOCATION: lat 49° 27' 33" N. long 02° 30' 58" W.

DEPTH: bottom 80'–85'. SURVEYS: subaqua.

ADDITIONAL: First reported in 1969. It has been discovered that this was a German type ammunition ship—so it is wise to stay away until this has been verified or otherwise.

Wreck 393. Unknown

LOCATION: lat 49° 27' 20" N. long 02° 30' 45" W.

DEPTH: bottom 100'.

ADDITIONAL: This wreck is marked on the charts as a 'foul', which is incorrect.

Wreck 394. Unknown

LOCATION: lat 49° 27' 26" N. long 02° 31' 04" W.

DEPTH: bottom 75'.

ADDITIONAL: This wreck is incorrectly marked as a 'foul' on the charts.

Wreck 395. BEAUPORT

LOCATION: lat 49° 27' 30" N. long 02° 31' 27" W. (E).

DEPTH: bottom 45'.

ADDITIONAL: This is an area of much wreckage from several ships. It is believed that one of these was the Beauport, but this is unconfirmed. The wreck area is approx. 200' × 60'.

Wreck 396. Unknown

LOCATION: lat 49° 26' 30" N. long 02° 31' 30" W.

DEPTH: least 10'. SURVEYS: subaqua.

ADDITIONAL: This is presumed to be a German vessel of approx. 4000 t. and 150' in length which sank during World War Two.

Wreck 397. British steamship DAGENHAM

DIMENSIONS: 239·3 × 36 × 15·5. TONNAGE: 1466 t.g.

BUILT: 1907. SINKING: 8th April 1909.

LOCATION: lat 49° 24' 55" N. long 02° 32' 10" W. (E).

ADDITIONAL: This vessel was stranded and broke in two.

105

Wreck 398. British steamship OCEAN QUEEN
DIMENSIONS: 151 × 24·1 × 11. TONNAGE: 421 t.g.
ROUTE: London–Guernsey. SINKING: 2nd March 1906.
LOCATION: lat 49° 25′ 20″ N. long 02° 39′ 00″ W. (A).
DEPTH: bottom 35′ approx.
ADDITIONAL: This vessel has never been located, although the position given should be correct. It was last seen on Cain's Rock, under the cliffs.

Wreck 399. Liberian motor vessel LA SALLE
TONNAGE: 5879 t.g. ROUTE: Port Lincoln–Hamburg.
CARGO: 9000 t. oats. SINKING: 28th May 1965.
LOCATION: lat 49° 29′ 16″ N. long 02° 39′ 21″ W. (E). Or, HSF, St Saviour's Church Tower, 31° 10′ to Fort Saumary Tower, 37° 47′ to Grande Etacre.
DEPTH: bottom 25′–30′. SURVEYS: RN; subaqua.
ADDITIONAL: The 2 t., four-bladed propeller was salvaged in 1969 by local subaqua divers.

Wreck 400. Steamship BRISEIS
DIMENSIONS: 320·6 × 45·9 × 23·1. TONNAGE: 2964 t.g.
BUILT: 1914. ROUTE: Oban–Rouen.
CARGO: wine. SINKING: 1st October 1937.
LOCATION: lat 49° 29′ 30″ N. long 02° 37′ 30″ W.
DEPTH: bottom 54′.
ADDITIONAL: This wreck is, at the time of writing, considered a danger to navigation. So it is possible that some efforts will be made to remove mast, funnels, etc.

INDEX

INDEX

111

WRECK NO.	NAME AND DATE OF SINKING	WRECK NO.	NAME AND DATE OF SINKING
125 128 132 133 134 137 138 142		135	Vittoria Claudia. 1963
144 151 154 158 160 165 166 167		8	Volnay. 1917
168 175 177 182 200 202 203 204		389	Voorwaarts. 1950
212 213 216 219 221 230 245 255		164	Wallsend. 1918
256 257 259 262 263 268 280 285		83	War Helmet. 1918
289 291 293 296 297 298 299 302		63	Westville. 1917
305 306 312 321 322 324 329 332		307	Whiteplain
340 343 346 356 357 371 374 381		303	Wiema. 1961
390 391 392 393 394 396		288	William Rhodes Moorhouse. 1968
192	Urlana. 1943		
185	U 81 German destroyer. 1919	228	Winsome. 1969
		21	Wreathier. 1917
248	Vedra. 1914	225	Zafiris. 1965
87	Vernon II. 1924	325	Zelo. 1920
242	Viking. 1889		

112